A
MONOCULAR
MEMOIR
A PILOT'S LIFE

MICHAEL WILLIAMS

FONTHILL

Fonthill Media Language Policy

Fonthill Media publishes in the international English language market. One language edition is published worldwide. As there are minor differences in spelling and presentation, especially with regard to American English and British English, a policy is necessary to define which form of English to use. The Fonthill Policy is to use the form of English native to the author. Michael Williams was born in Pembrokeshire, Wales, and now lives in Wiltshire therefore British English has been adopted in this publication.

Fonthill Media Limited
Fonthill Media LLC
www.fonthillmedia.com
office@fonthillmedia.com

First published in the United Kingdom
and the United States of America 2016

British Library Cataloguing in Publication Data:
A catalogue record for this book is available from the British Library

ISBN 978-1-78155-563-7

Typeset in 11pt on 13pt Sabon
Printed and bound by CPI Group (UK) Ltd, Croydon, CR0 4YY

A
MONOCULAR
MEMOIR

Foreword
by
Air Chief Marshal Sir Michael Graydon GCB CBE RAF Retd

For those of my generation, this short but delightful memoir of Mike Williams life and times will stir many memories. Cranwellians of the late 1950s and early 60s engaged in their jet conversion to Vampires will recall a good looking and sympathetic instructor who had the time and sense to make this testing time a pleasure rather than a trial. Mike stood out then as a man with charm and style.

Throughout his career, Mike retained that charm and easy going approach which made him so popular in the Royal Air Force, with the other services and in the civilian world. But behind that aura lay a great professionalism and strength of character, so necessary for a test pilot, the operations floor at the Ministry of Defence and Station Commander at the Central Flying School. Without that inner core of steel, it is unlikely he would have continued to fly after the loss of one eye, and in the process become something of a legend.

Looking through his Record of Service, from 1954 Initial Training at Kirton Lindsey to his retirement as Deputy Commandant at Cranwell 1984, one is struck by the number of bases no longer in being with the RAF. Kirton Lindsey, Middleton St George, Chivenor, Stradishall, Waterbeach, Little Rissington, Aden, Manby—all of them in their day lively, important stations and ones which had a profound influence on the many young men and women who spent time there. The ghosts of those days peep out from the pages of this book. They bear witness to just how great the changes have been to the RAF and how much smaller it is today.

It would be easy to suggest that the era Mike Williams describes was more fun, more varied and more interesting than the essentially UK based service of today despite the fact that the RAF has been almost permanently on operations abroad since 1991. In reality, the world has changed and the armed services have had to change with it. But young men and women still join the military for much the same reason as did Mike, and they still get the satisfaction from achievements in the air and on the ground as did he. What I hope those of the modern generation who read this book will learn is that professionalism can accommodate graciousness and charm, a life outside the service without in any way compromising excellence.

Mike Williams' career was a model for this and his influence on so many he met along with that of Jackie his wife is exemplified by the smile that can be guaranteed whenever the Williams name is mentioned. A lovely book which I know you will enjoy.

CONTENTS

Acknowledgements

In writing this book I have had generous help from many people and I am particularly grateful to Air Chief Marshal Sir Michael James Graydon GCB, CBE, RAF Retd, for writing the Foreword; to Patricia Forrest GAvA, for the use of her wonderful painting of 'my' Hunter; and to all the following for their advice and support: Wing Commander J. A. 'Robby' Robinson AFC, FRAeS, RAF Retd; Bruce Gauntlett; The IWM; The Boscombe Down Aviation Museum; Tim Pierce, the Assistant Librarian at The Royal Air Force College Cranwell; The Museum of Army Flying; The Buckingham Palace Press Office; The National Archives in relation to Crown Copyright; and to all my family who insisted that I write this memoir in the first place and have done so much typing, research and proof reading.

Most of the photos were taken by myself and we have made every effort to trace copyright of those which are not. If you believe you are the owner of any of these images and we have not requested your permission to use them, please contact us.

1

Early Years

I was born on the 9th of August 1929 in a town house in Haverfordwest, Pembrokeshire the son of a country solicitor. Pembrokeshire was mainly a farming and fishing county, particularly known for its early potatoes. I was joined by my brother David some four years later and shortly after that we moved to a larger house in Dale Road, Haverfordwest. This became our family home for the next 25 years. We were a comfortably off family and as most middle class did in those days we employed a gardener and help in the house, the latter was provided by girls who came to the town mainly from the farms and they 'lived in' as there was not much public transport and certainly not many people had their own car.

In due course I was sent to school at Hill House College in the town, a small private establishment run by Miss Agnes and Miss Mildred. My brother David some four years younger than me tended to inherit my clothes when I had finished with them and one day my mother presented brother David at Hill House College. Miss Agnes or was it Miss Mildred said, 'That's a nice coat David' and he said, 'Yes thank you it was Michael's before me'. My mother, thinking that hand-me-downs were perhaps beneath our social standing, was not pleased.

I have few memories of the school but it served to teach me the '3Rs' and I eventually went on to board at a prep school in the Cotswolds. I had been there for a year when war broke out and my Father—convinced that invasion was imminent—as were many people in 1940—brought me back home because he wanted all the family together.

Eventually I returned to the prep school, which like many others at the time, was run along strict, almost 'boot camp' lines. As I was, even at that age, something of a rebel especially to the extent of openly disliking cricket—a passion of the headmaster—I did not enjoy my years there and when the time came to leave I happily moved on to Marlborough College, in Wiltshire. Although the war meant that times were hard, this school suited me much better. Many of the younger masters had been called up to fight so we were taught by retired men who had returned to fill the vacancies created by this situation. I am afraid that, boys being boys, we gave some of these very admirable men a hard time. We all happily joined 'The Corps' and were allowed a great deal of freedom to shoot our 303 rifles on the open range. Going shooting in the afternoon enabled me to avoid cricket, which I never played again after prep school. Riding our bikes through the Wiltshire countryside, swimming in the outdoor, unheated pool, (at that age we didn't feel the cold) and tobogganing down Granham Hill were great sports and the latter was responsible for the loss of two of my front teeth! Another school memory is standing in the street watching the American tanks roll through the town on the way to the D-Day landings. The American troops threw us sweets, a real treat in rationed Britain. I made many lasting friendships at Marlborough some of which continue to this day.

National Service and University

When I left Marlborough in 1947 aged 18 with a handful of school certificates. National Service was in full swing and I joined the Army with the intention of serving in my Father's old regiment, The Welch Regiment. Accordingly when called up in August of that year I reported to No. 28 Infantry Training Battalion at Palace Barracks, Hollywood, Northern Ireland. The Spartan living conditions came as no shock to me compared with prep school, but too many young men who had never been away from home it was a traumatic experience. I soon decided that infantry soldiering was not for me and I opted to transfer to the Royal Armoured Corps. This resulted in a posting to a training regiment in Catterick where I learned to drive tanks amongst other such useful skills. Having been earmarked as a possible officer I duly moved on to Mons Officer Cadet training unit at Aldershot. Mons was, at that time, under the authoritarian command of Regimental Sergeant Major (RSM) Brittain. Brittain was adept at putting the fear of God into people and we lived in dread of displeasing him as we knew this meant ending up in the guard room on a charge.

I had hoped to be sent, on commissioning, to an armoured regiment, but the Royal Artillery suddenly needed a lot more subalterns and I was sent, as a 2nd Lieutenant, to the 49th Regiment RA at Norton Barracks Worcester.

The 49th had 3 batteries, one with towed 17 pounder anti-tank guns, another with self-propelled 17 pounders mounted on the Valentine tank chassis and the 3rd battery was devoted to training National Service men on 25 pounders.

The 49th was a happy regiment, although having a total of eleven National Service subalterns its main concern was, perhaps, not soldiering but keeping the troops usefully occupied.

My main means of transport at the time of National Service was a motorbike but I did eventually get my first car, a Morris 8 Tourer. At this time driving tests had not been re-introduced after the war so I got a motorcycle licence with no need for a test.

As they were to reintroduce driving tests and I did not have a car licence, I discovered that regulations at the time allowed an Army driving licence to be converted automatically to a civil car licence. Seeing this as an easy option I thought this would be a good way to approach the problem so I badgered the Military Transport Officer to agree to give me a car test.

Eventually he relented and said 'OK meet me at my office next Monday morning'. This I duly did and he said. 'Oh Mike I am far too busy look at this' pointing at a huge pile of files in his in-tray.

I said 'Oh come on you did promise'.

He relented and said 'Oh alright, have you got something to take the test in?'

I said 'yes', he said 'what is it?'

I said 'it's a Quad', which was a four wheel drive vehicle used to tow guns, a horrible piece of machinery with very heavy steering and a crash gear box.

He said 'a Quad?'

I said 'well that's all your MT section would let me have'.

He said 'where is it?'

I said 'outside your office'.

He said 'how did it get there?'

I said 'I drove it'.

He said 'you drove it down here from the MT section?'

I said 'yes.'

He said 'well then you have passed; congratulations.' So this is how I got a full driving licence—without ever taking a test!

I personally found time to play sport, mainly rugby, on three afternoons a week. At this point I seriously considered making a career in the Army but decided that it was not for me; mainly because at that time the Army had so much time tied up with training National Service men. It was in fact a very lucky decision not to stay in the 49th as a short time later they were sent out to Korea and were badly knocked about losing many officers and men.

What to do next was the obvious question. I decided that a university degree would be useful. In those days many people took a University College entrance exam while still at school and had their entry to University deferred until they had finished National Service. I had not done this, so I had to take on a programme of applying to Universities. To assist me in the college entrance exams I would have to sit I embarked on a short course at a crammer in London.

The nearest convenient digs were part of the London Musical Club in Holland Park. One of the other residents was a very pretty young actress named Jane Griffiths who had recently appeared in a film with Gregory Peck called *The Million Pound Note*. Jane had many admirers of more substantial means than me although I found her very attractive. One day in an uninitiated fit of curiosity I asked Jane what it was like being kissed by Gregory Peck, she replied 'not as nice as you my dear'. Although probably more attributable to kindness than veracity it cheered me up for some days!

I applied to a number of colleges, mostly at Oxford, and was eventually offered places at Worcester College and University College. The courses there would have started in autumn 1951 which would have meant losing another year; I declined these offers and opted, with the encouragement of a school colleague who was already there, to go to Trinity College, Dublin (TCD) in 1950. It was not until a year had passed that I realised that the TCD law course lasted four years, as opposed to three years at Oxford so I lost a year anyway! At that time everyone assumed that after qualifying as a solicitor I would join the family firm (R. T. P. Williams and Sons) in Haverfordwest with a view to eventually practising with my father and first cousin Howell, this was never to transpire as will be revealed later.

The law course at TCD was a disappointment, containing as it did a large slice of Irish law which differed from British law in some crucial respects. This, of course is something I should have discovered before embarking on my studies! I did enjoy my time in Dublin even if it was not scholastically useful. Once I had decided to cease my law studies the best option seemed to be to press on and get a pass arts degree rather than to have nothing to show for my time at Trinity. I eventually achieved a pass degree BA which was, on payment of a small sum of money, upgraded to an MA after three unblemished years.

One of my fondest memories of my time in Dublin was the amount of rugby I was able to play in the considerable spare time that my dilatory academic studies permitted. One of my first interests on arriving at Trinity was to find out how to get involved with the Rugby Club. It became obvious, by observation and discussions with others that the TCD Rugby Club was heavily biased in favour of students reading medicine or hailing from the North of Ireland. I therefore looked around the other senior league clubs in Dublin and, by accident, got an introduction to Monkstown RFC. The result was that on an early Saturday I played in one of the lower teams, presumably by way of a trial. To my surprise the following Saturday I found myself carded to play in the first fifteen. I played in that team for most of the rest of the season until after Christmas when I decided that I should limit my Rugby and do some academic work. As a result of this decision, which was a disappointment to the club because of their upcoming league competition matches in January, I was demoted to the travelling 1st team. This I saw as no disadvantage because it meant travelling to play teams in other parts of the Republic and also Northern Ireland.

Back home during the long summer vacation I came under pressure from my mother to earn some money and I went to the job centre and was offered a job driving the NAAFI van at the Royal Naval Air Station, Brawdy, where the main unit based there was 806 Squadron flying Sea Hawks. The van was a pretty hideous affair powered by an unreliable Ford V8 engine. Its main problem was starting first thing in the morning. The van stood outside overnight so if the morning was at all damp firing up the engine was difficult. On running late I would get a lot of stick from the Naval ratings along the lines of 'what Fxxing time do you call this, Taff?' it was all good natured and understandable but something I had difficulty rectifying. In fact I never did manage to get the damn thing to start reliably but the teasing from the ratings when I was late got steadily more good natured. The money was no better than the machinery as was to be expected, but it did help to fund my early attempts at trout fishing which started mainly in the local river Cleddau, during those vacation summers. I was fortunate in that a family friend owned a sizeable stretch of the river at Trefgarne near home where I had permanent permission to fish. The river had a run of salmon and sea trout and I caught very little, until one day spinning in a large pool I hooked my first salmon, he had obviously been in the river some time, trying to get up to spawn and I felt so sorry for him I put him back, but it ignited my passion for fishing which lasted well on into life, to be revitalised in a big way when I was posted to Boscombe Down in 1963. There the Officers' Mess had access to considerable fishing mainly on the Upper Avon, a classic chalk stream, then under the control and care of the famous river keeper Frank Sawyer.

2

Beginning of Flying Career

My interest in flying did not start as early in life as it seemed to for many of my RAF colleagues. Alan Cobham, the great showman, and his flying circus visited Haverfordwest occasionally during my early youth, in the 1930s. He would operate from a field inside the old racecourse close to our house in Dale Road. I certainly went to watch, fascinated. My first cousin, Richard, actually went up as a passenger in one of the circus's planes on one occasion and this sparked his interest to the point where he flew Spitfires in the Second World War.

My interest in flying on the other hand was awakened in the late 1950s, during my time at Trinity College, partly by the fact that at that time the Fleet Air Arm was advertising widely for pilots and partly due to socialising on the odd evening with the pilots of 806 Squadron, Fleet Air Arm which was stationed at Brawdy airfield near my home in Pembrokeshire.

During the vacations from university we used to meet with their pilots at one or other of the little hostelries, perhaps the Mariners in Haverfordwest or the Ship Inn in Solva. 806 Squadron flew the Sea Hawk which was a nice little lightweight fighter, a predecessor of the Hunter. The Royal Air Force was not actively seeking pilots at that time because it had many capable experienced and distinguished aviators left over from the Second World War and probably, in fact, not enough cockpits for them to occupy. I therefore applied to join the Fleet Air Arm as a pilot. After exhaustive tests at Royal Naval Air Station Lee on Solent I met for a final interview with a naval commander.

He said 'Right Williams! You have passed all the tests and we will accept you for training as a pilot or observer.'

I said: 'What is this "or observer" bit? I only want to be a pilot!'

The commander said: 'You will be a pilot if you pass the pilot training.'

'But what if I fail the pilot training?'

'In that case you will have to go on to be an observer.'

'But I only want to be a pilot. If I fail the pilot training can I leave?'

'No, you would have to go on to be an observer.'

'So I can't leave if I fail the pilot training?'

'No!'

'I'm sorry, that is not acceptable.'

The commander made no further comment, possibly seeing in me someone who might be prepared to precipitate a difficult situation by deliberately failing the observer training if forced in that direction. As a result of this exchange I applied to the Royal Air Force which is probably what I should have done in the first place!

The RAF subjected me to another series of tests, firstly two days flying aptitude at RAF Hornchurch and then another two days Officer Selection at Daedalus House, RAF College Cranwell. The latter consisted of interviews, leadership and team exercises and at the end I was offered an immediate permanent position with antedates of seniority for my university degree and my time of commissioned service in the Army and best of all, if I failed my flying training I would be allowed to leave immediately with no subsequent commitments—so I signed up.

My main memory of this stay at Cranwell was watching the Balliol aircraft doing circuits, at the time the RAF was looking to overhaul its flying training syllabus and was assessing aircraft to follow on from the Harvard. The Balliol was initially considered but in the event a change of mind meant that all through jet training was introduced starting with the Jet Provost and proceeding onto advanced training on the Vampire.

Flying training

My initial posting was to No. 1 Initial Training School at Kirton Lindsey in Lincolnshire, there I learned about the RAF in general and in particular its differences from the Army and a little about its history etc. Initial flying training came next at RAF Hullavington between Chippenham and Malmesbury in Wiltshire. At the time initial flying training was undertaken on the Provost T1, a low wing monoplane with a decent 550 hp Alvis Leonides engine. It proved unexpectedly challenging. I did not realise there was so much involved. So many controls, right foot, right side of rudder bar to turn right, opposite to motorbikes especially when trying to taxi, but it passed uneventfully. I found myself on a course whose other members had all been on university air squadrons and they were way ahead of me in general airmanship matters, such as the range of maps in use at the time; despite this I went solo successfully after about eight hours dual, which was around the norm and I completed the course on schedule.

After training on the Piston Provost at Hullavington in Wiltshire I moved up to Middleton Saint George near Darlington to fly the Vampire. No. 4 Flight Training School (FTS) had a mixture of Vampire T11 two-seaters and single-seater Vampire FB5s. The form was that one did dual sorties with an instructor in the T11 two-seater before being sent off solo in the T11. Subsequently one was seated in a single-seat FB5 Vampire and sent off to fly solo. It is a curious fact that on several occasions students who had performed well during their training on the Provost and had gone solo in the T11 Vampire two-seater failed to solo in the FB5. Several taxied out to the beginning of the runway and then taxied back to dispersal. Strangely they could not face flying alone in the single-seater. It could have been the fact that the FB5 did feel very different because it was so much smaller, you were patently so alone in the cockpit without any side-by-side seating, or maybe that it was not fitted with ejector seats, as was the T11. I cannot guess at the mental processes of the students who chickened-out of flying, those that did taxi back in without taking off did not get a second chance and were sent home with LMF Low Moral Fibre on their reports. With great relief I completed my first solo in the Vampire T11 on 25 July 1955 and followed it three days later with my first solo in the FB5. I was awarded my wings in March 1956. I was nominated to take the passing out parade as having been in the Army knew a bit about sword drill.

At the end of my Vampire training at Middleton Saint George in March 1956 I was posted on to a Hunter course at Chivenor, near Barnstable, North Devon. After a few dual sorties in a Vampire T11 we were sent off solo in a Mark 1 Hunter single-seater. At this time there were no twin-seat Hunters and no simulator so we sat in the cockpit on the ground to sort out where the controls were and off we went! The performance of the Hunter 1 with very little fuel and 7,500 pounds of thrust from the engine was a revelation to Vampire pilots and my first solo in a Hunter was much more memorable than my first solo in a Provost had been. The rate of climb was sensational and the controls with power assistance were very light. Such was the acceleration that several students failed to raise their undercarriage before getting to 10,000 feet! I enjoyed flying the Hunter 1 enormously even though its lack of fuel was a hindrance, limiting the length of sorties to little over 30 minutes in most cases. Later versions of the Hunter were fitted with external drop tanks to carry more fuel and some, such as the Mark 6, were fitted with the more powerful Rolls Royce Avon 200 series engine which also improved the performance.

The Hunter course proceeded pleasurably during the summer of 1956, which saw a heat wave and when off duty we were able to take full advantage of the magnificent beaches close to the airfield. At the time I was driving a vintage low chassis 2 litre Lagonda, which for some strange reason, seemed to attract young ladies, so it was altogether a very happy summer with daily flying in the Hunter to liven things up.

One feature of life then was that we were often able to borrow an aircraft for the weekend on payment of 10 shillings into the coffee fund. A colleague and I had several weekends in London courtesy of borrowing a Vampire T11 and leaving it at Biggin Hill for the weekend. This worked very well and the flying was booked as training, which of course it was. The halcyon days of booking out an aircraft for the weekend ended when flying hours became more and more expensive.

At the end of the Hunter course at Chivenor our postings came in. I was bitterly disappointed to be the only student on the course not posted to a Hunter squadron. I was posted to Number 245 Squadron at Stradishall in Suffolk flying Meteor 8s instead. In fact and with the benefit of hindsight the posting to Meteors was no bad thing and I can now see that perhaps the thinking was that as an older than average pilot on the course, perhaps more mature and responsible, I might cope better with an in squadron conversion to asymmetric flying, that is flying on one engine out of two. Number 245 Squadron at Stradishall was the last Meteor squadron in Fighter Command, because all the others had already been converted to Hunters.

3

Squadron Life

245 Squadron was in fact great fun. The Meteor F8 with which the squadron was equipped was pleasant and undemanding to fly and the major role for the squadron was 'rat and terrier' work mainly undertaken at low level. The squadron also possessed a two-seater Meteor Mark 7, used for instruction purposes and instrument ratings. My conversion to the Meteor was conducted by the Wing Commander Flying (WCF) at Stradishall who saw it as an opportunity to get some flying hours in for himself.

Although the Meteor 8 was pleasant and easy to fly the lack of performance was disappointing when compared with the Hunter. Within a short time of my arrival on 245 Squadron it was announced that the squadron was to be re-equipped with Hunters. This did in fact begin to happen with the stores getting in a stock of Hunter spares while at the same time it was announced that the squadron was shortly to disband. So by a miracle of joined-up planning, the squadron was at the same time re-equipping with Hunters and planning for its disbandment. I did the odd trip in a 245 Squadron Hunter, a Mark 4, and suffered one occasion when, on landing, the brakes on one wheel failed and I went straight on at the end of the runway, through the boundary hedge. I had resisted the temptation to raise the undercarriage, reasoning that it would cause more damage to the aircraft and probably me if I did.

Eventually we ended up, undercarriage and flaps down, in a ploughed field which slowed the aircraft down nicely! The photos show the aircraft in the field and the hole in the hedge it passed through. After initially being accused of landing too fast I was fortunate to be able to point to a chewed up starboard brake as evidence of a technical failure.

Suez

My time happily flying on 245 Squadron was interrupted by two episodes both connected with the 1956 Suez operation. First I was posted on detachment to 215 Wing at RAF Yatesbury in Wiltshire, to join a mobile wing which was building up to go into a captured Egyptian airfield to operate it as a transport support air head and also as a fighter ground attack base.

We were made very welcome at Yatesbury which was then a radio training establishment and during our time there the Officers' mess decided to have their summer ball and 215 Wing was invited with its guests. I recall that during the ball at around midnight I went to the bar to organise a replenishment of champagne only to be told that they had run out of the two dozen bottles that they had stocked up for the ball and no more were available. They clearly had not foreseen the consumption by 215 Wing who had dealt with most of the bottles until then.

The build-up to the Suez operation was bedevilled by frequent changes of plan at high level and 215 Wing set up a rumour board one of which read 'no news yet, but don't buy any long playing records'. Eventually plans changed to the point where 215 Wing was no longer needed and I returned to 245 Squadron.

I note from items on the internet that the airfield in Egypt, Gamil near Port Said, from where 215 were intended to operate was eventually captured by British and French Para troops, however by this time 215 Wing in the UK had been disbanded.

The next interlude was during the actual build-up to the Suez operation when I was posted out to the War Headquarters at Episkopi in Cyprus as an ops officer. After a comfortable flight out in a civil DC4 snuggled up to a comely air hostess I arrived in Cyprus on the very day that the war ended. I spent the next few weeks running the waiting list for flights home to the UK. My brother who was then serving in the Army with a Royal Artillery Regiment at Colchester also suffered from the disorganisation. He was sent off from Colchester with most of the MT and drivers from his regiment to board ship and go to Port Said. When he arrived and reported in at the end of a sickening voyage through the Bay of Biscay he was told that the rest of his regiment was still in Colchester and so he was not required. He spent the next few weeks on the telephone to me trying to get a flight back to the UK. I was unable to give him sufficient priority on a long waiting list which included myself, so he eventually returned to the UK on a deafening flight in a Shackleton.

Another incident worth recording from my time on 245 Squadron was my experience of an engine failure in a Meteor 8. Having been launched one day on an exercise interception of a raid by Canberra's simulating the enemy I was cruising happily at full power at about 30,000 ft trailing a Canberra when I noticed the RPM on one of the engines fluctuating, this continued until the engine flamed out. The recommended procedure for a relight required a descent to below 20,000 ft. Descending as necessary and heading towards base I shut the high pressure cock as required and then tried to open it again with the relight button pressed. Unfortunately I could not fully open the hp cock which had jammed at about half way along its travel. This effectively precluded a relight. I optimistically continued to try to clear the blockage by pulling hard on the hp cock until eventually it snapped and I was left holding the broken end of the relight button.

I had kept Air Traffic Control at Stradishall informed of the problem and they conveniently cleared the circuit of other aircraft and declared a state of emergency 'Sprog pilot with engine failure'.

I was determined at all costs to avoid getting low and slow with only one engine working and therefore set up for a glide approach. Fortunately the weather was good with unlimited visibility and a gentle headwind blowing straight down the runway. The landing was uneventful and I was able to taxi to dispersal on one engine.

My account of the incident was not originally believed and I was accused of inciting the flame out by hammering the throttles. This was in a way understandable as the engineers had not been able to find any fault with the engine. Eventually the engineers identified an intermittent fault in the relevant fuel pump and I was exonerated. I was told later that the breaking strain of the hp cock had been tested and was 1½ tons so I had obviously been very keen to achieve a relight!

Eventually my next posting arrived and I was sent to No. 63 Squadron at RAF Waterbeach near Cambridge. This was really good news as 63 flew Hunter 6s which were a vast improvement in that they had the more powerful 200 series Rolls Royce Avon engines which gave vastly improved performance.

4

Waterbeach Target Practice

Target practice was a regular part of our training at Waterbeach. Targets, called 'flags' made out of a 9 ft rectangle of hessian would be towed on steel cables behind a tug aircraft flying at about 10,000 ft into an air-firing range. This was usually over the sea, and in our case was out in the Wash area. Each pilot's shells were coated in paint of a different colour. The tug plane would fly back to base and release the shot 'flag' with its shell holes, over the airfield. The hessian rectangle would be retrieved and reviewed as to how many hits each pilot had scored by counting the coloured holes in the fabric. Unfortunately the shells could damage the tug cables holding the target and the target would sometimes drop off before the tug had the chance to get back to the airfield.

One particular night, after we had flown several Hunters to fire at the target we were all back at base. Unfortunately the flag had been lost so nobody had any way of knowing how many hits they had scored.

Our flight commander, Dan Hill, was incandescent, as he believed he had had a really good shoot.

'I really clobbered that flag it must be riddled with brown holes,' he said. The rest of us looked at each other exasperated until one of the more mischievous of us, Buster Skinner, had an idea and snuck out of the room. Next thing the telephone rang. A call had come through to the squadron from someone asking to speak to the person in charge.

The flight commander, Dan, left off talking about his lost triumph to answer the phone.

'Hello I'm the flight commander in charge, what can I do for you?'

'PC Clutterbuck here of Little Snoring in Norfolk, it is near Norwich, you know' said a thickly accented voice on the other end.

'Yes I know where Little Snoring is....' said the commander.

'I think we may have found something that belongs to you....' said the PC.

'Is it a flag?' Dan interrupted, seeing a chance to prove his prowess after all.

'No it's not a flag, it is a long bit of hessian with a black circle.'

'Yes that's a flag.'

'No sir it's not a flag, it's got no stars or stripes on it.'

The flight commander switched on his the speakerphone now, seeing a chance to prove his point.

'We have it safe, your flag that isn't a flag. It's locked in the cell' said the PC.

'Has it got any holes in it?'

'I don't know sir.'

'Can you look at it?'

'Err yes I can go and have a look at it.' The phone went quiet for a while until the PC returned to it with the flag, which was not a flag.

'Has it got any holes in it? I am particularly interested in brown holes,' said the excited Dan.

'Brown holes you say Sir!'

'Yes, brown holes!'

'Brown holes?'

By this time we were all laughing uncontrollably and the ruse was up and Buster Skinner returned from the other room to a massive roar of approval.

The flight commander, Dan, who never found his brown holes, went on to be an Air Chief Marshal and I went on to try to develop better target systems which will be retold later.

In the summer of 1957 I was sent to Chivenor to do the Hunter simulator course. I stalled on the first three take-offs despite having already flown around 50 hours on the actual aircraft. Whilst discussing my next simulator sortie asked the instructor

'Could I please try a landing?'

He said 'what do you mean; you have already done two sorties.'

I replied 'Yes but in both them you built up the emergencies to the point where I had to eject!'

It is noteworthy that my first simulator landing attempt was no more successful than early take-offs had been; naturally the fault was in the simulator. This goes to show how unrepresentative simulators were in those early days.

While I was with 63 Squadron on the Hunter 6s I was detailed to take an aircraft down to London Airport (now Heathrow) for a static display for Battle of Britain weekend in September 1958. I took off in my Hunter and contacted London Airport who were very efficient and fed me into their landing pattern. This involved flying over central London on the approach to one of their western runways at a height of 1,500 feet above ground level with flaps and under-carriage down. In a single engine aircraft this felt somewhat uncomfortable and I pondered on what action I would take if the engine suddenly failed. I was sitting on an ejection seat so would no doubt have survived but what concerned me was what would happen to the aircraft once I got out of it. At the time I thought it probable that the best thing to do might be to point the aircraft into an unpopulated area and leave ejection until the last minute. Hyde Park and the Serpentine seemed a possible option. Fortunately the engine, being by Rolls Royce, continued to behave impeccably, for there was no procedure written to cover such an unusual situation.

On the Saturday of the Battle of Britain weekend I had to stand duty in my best uniform next to the aircraft to greet spectators and answer any questions. A ladder was attached to the side of the aircraft to enable access to the cockpit but it was well understood that no spectator should be allowed into the cockpit because of a danger of loose objects being dropped which could jam controls on subsequent flights. Unfortunately for me a very smart and glamorous Pan Am stewardess arrived and begged to be allowed into the cockpit. My iron resolve weakened and I allowed her to climb up the access ladder to get into the cockpit. She was dressed in a smart uniform with split skirt when, having got one foot in and with the other still on the ladder she announced she was stuck. So I had to climb the ladder and grapple with her to help her into the cockpit to the delight of a growing crowd. Eventually I managed to get her in, and back out and down the ladder to a round of applause from a delighted crowd. That day I learned a valuable lesson about trusting my judgement.

Parked in the enclosure with the Hunter was a Blackburn Beverley. It was the first time I had seen such a monster and little did I realise how much time I would spend flying one as a test pilot during my tour at Boscombe Down.

On the next Monday morning after a careful check for any loose objects in the cockpit, I called London Airport who offered to send out a truck to guide me back to the active runway because London Airport's runways and taxiways are a maze. I was asked how fast I would like the truck to travel and told they had had a Canberra in the week before that went at 50 miles an hour. I said '40 mph please' and set off behind the FOLLOW ME air traffic truck which may or may not have been doing 40 mph. Either way, I could not keep up with him and he had to slow down.

Take off on London Airport's 9,000 ft runway was no problem and it was a joy to be able to do a virtually vertical climb out of the airport and set heading for Waterbeach.

The other squadron based at Waterbeach was 56 Squadron which had a long and distinguished flying history. They were equipped with Hunter 5s which were fitted with the Armstrong Siddeley Sapphire engine. I scrounged a trip in one of their planes and remember the Sapphire was less powerful than the Hunter 6 Avon engine and it had disconcerting habit of emitting groaning sounds at regular intervals, I did not particularly enjoy the flight although I was grateful to 56 Squadron for allowing me one.

After about a year on 63 Squadron it was announced that the squadron would be disbanding. This was a great disappointment for me since the Hunter 6 was probably the best mark of Hunter, certainly the best mark that I had flown. When it came time for 63 to disband it was the top performing squadron in Fighter Command and its aircraft were transferred to 56 Squadron, a lower order although more historic unit. This caused considerable disillusionment among the members of 63 Squadron.

5

Flying Instructor Little Rissington and Cranwell

The question then arose as to what I would do next. The officer at Fighter Command, in charge of my posting, rang me up and said: 'You have quite a lot of seniority as Flight Lieutenant and you have not got very many flying hours'. He said: 'I am going to get you a job that will give you plenty of flying hours'. I then got a posting notice to join a squadron based at Aldergrove in Northern Ireland.

The squadron's role was to fly exploratory meteorological flights in Hastings aircraft. I hastily arranged to fly a Vampire over to Aldergrove to visit my soon-to-be new squadron. What I found was not very encouraging. To become a captain would take about 18 months of flying as second pilot, with responsibility for raising and lowering the undercarriage and flaps. This did not seem a very attractive option for a steely-eyed fighter pilot so I got in my Vampire and flew full-throttle home, leaving that posting to some other unfortunate fighter pilot.

On arrival back at Waterbeach I promptly submitted an application to take a flying instructor's course. There must have been very few volunteers to be flying instructors at that time because almost immediately I was posted to The Central Flying School (CFS) at RAF Little Rissington in Gloucestershire in September 1958 to undertake the training.

Central Flying School was formed at Upavon in 1912 to train professional war pilots. In 1920 CFS amalgamated with the School of Special Flying with the primary aim to train flying instructors for the Royal Air Force. In 1946 CFS moved to Little Rissington where it stayed until 1976 when they moved to Cranwell where they continue to train Flying Instructors for all three services and many foreign countries.

The Armorial bearings of the Central Flying School which were awarded in 1931 feature a Pelican and the motto '*Imprimis Praecepta*'—'Our Teaching is Everlasting'. Her Majesty the Queen presented CFS with the Queen's Colour in 1969. Queen Elizabeth the Queen Mother had a long association with CFS as their Commandant in Chief from 1960 until her death.

The late 50s were a tough time, with squadrons disbanding everywhere. RAF Germany was also contracting so the number of jobs for single-seater fighter pilots was diminishing fast. The reason there were so few volunteers to be instructors in those days was possibly because there was a widespread feeling that once you got into the training machine they would not readily let you go and you would find it difficult to get back to operational flying again. I did not really see that my role in life was to kill people so I was not worried by that.

I had mixed feelings about the CFS course—the ground school in particular which put a lot of emphasis on remembering such useless information as the rotational speed of the various gyro instruments in the plane—which could not in any case be adjusted in the cockpit. The 'in air' flying instruction which taught us how to teach was much more relevant and I realised that the best way to learn about flying was by learning how to teach it.

During the course my Father died and I had to spend several weeks at home sorting out his affairs. I did not feel that that the ground school bits of the course that I missed were any great loss!

During the first part of the flying instructor training at Central Flying School (CFS) Little Rissington one was given the option of being an instructor in basic flying, which would mean instructing on small piston-engined aircraft, or instructing on the advanced jet training side which would mean flying Vampires. My decision was to remain in the jet side and go to a Vampire station. On graduation the Vampire volunteers were given a choice of three possible postings, one of which was RAF Cranwell. The general feeling was that Cranwell would provide too much of the peripheral bullshit, parades etc., possibly at the expense of the flying. This did not disturb me given my background of national service in the Army . I opted again for the less popular route at Cranwell and was accepted in February 1959. In hindsight, this was another good choice.

RAF College Cranwell

My first impression of Cranwell was how flat the land was coming from Little Rissington in the Cotswolds. In those days Cranwell ran the flight cadet courses which provided the future senior officers for the RAF.

There had been an airfield at Cranwell since the Navy opened the Central Training Establishment for the Royal Naval Air Service in 1916 as HMS *Daedalus*. After the war the Chief of the Air Staff; Air Chief Marshal Sir Hugh Trenchard was determined that the new Royal Air Force should have its own Officer Training College to rival Dartmouth and Sandhurst and RAF College Cranwell opened in February 1920. The main building College Hall was officially opened by the then Prince of Wales on 11 October 1934.

Those wishing to join the RAF could apply to become a cadet at Cranwell, but had to meet certain standards of academic achievement. By the time I arrived in February 1959 the College was well established with two entries of some 50 to 60 cadets arriving each year in January and September. At that time the qualification was a General Certificate of Education in subjects including English, Maths and Science or a foreign language plus two others and two passes at A level in subjects other than English, Handicrafts, Domestic Science, Art and Music which were excluded. The cadets would spend their first year on mainly academic studies, including Aeronautical Science, Engineering,

Humanities and General Service subjects. The second year on basic flying training on the Piston Provost and their third and final year on advanced flying training on the jet powered Vampire, the latter was where I came in.

They eventually left in the July or December three years later with a formal passing out parade usually reviewed by a member of the Royal Family, a Government Minister, Local Dignitary or Senior Military Officer. On these occasions they were joined by proud parents and friends for lunch in College Hall and a Ball in the evening.

I managed to get out of many of the parades by volunteering to do the fly-past which took off from Barkston Heath airfield a few miles away and returned there, thus avoiding having to get into best blue and meeting and greeting!

My role at Cranwell was basically to convert the cadets from the piston engine Provost to the Jet Vampire. Most of the flying was done in the two-seat Vampire T11 with some solo flying in the Vampire 5s and 9s which were single-seaters. Days were split into half a day flying and half a day ground school, with the odd bit of night flying and formation flying thrown in for each course.

One developed a fairly close relationship with some of the cadets, particularly those with whom one flew most often and it was encouraging how many very good young men were entering the service. It was fascinating to fly with, and teach, so many young men who subsequently went on to high ranks in the Service. One pleasant feature was that the cadets were basically happier being with us and flying rather than being in ground school.

During this time at Cranwell my interest in game shooting was renewed. There was a shoot which took place on the land surrounding the North and South airfields. This could be quite productive, I enjoyed that aspect very much and it led to some lasting friendships with locals such as Cis Bristow and his wife Mabel who lived on the edge of the airfield and farmed some of the Air Ministry land and Simon and Jane Wright, also a farmer whose family were old friends of my future wife.

Another interest was in motor cars and rallying in a minor way. The local motor club, which conducted rallies and things like driving tests

CENTRAL FLYING SCHOOL

𝕿𝖍𝖎𝖘 𝖎𝖘 𝖙𝖔 𝕮𝖊𝖗𝖙𝖎𝖋𝖞 *that*

Flight Lieutenant M.R.Williams

has successfully graduated from the

Central Flying School

as a Qualified Flying Instructor

DATE *19 Feb 59* COMMANDANT

F Flight, 3 Squadron, Instructors and Cadets Cranwell 1959.

was called the Poachers Motor Club and I joined, happily becoming involved in a little rally driving and also in planning rallies. In those days there were not nearly as many restrictions as there are today and rallies would take place on public roads although any timed sections had to be on private land. Success or failure usually depended mainly on good navigation.

It was during my involvement in the Poachers Motor Club that I met my wife to be, Jackie Edwards. There was a rally one Sunday, which I had half intended to enter but I did not get out of bed in time to register at the start point. I knew the rough area in which the rally was to take place and so I got in the car and drove around thinking to myself I am pretty sure to find a checkpoint in a layby somewhere and then I could find out at which pub the rally was ending and join the party there.

Coming round a corner I spotted an Austin Healy Sprite in a layby. I recognised it as belonging to a club member, Spike Hughes, and stopped to find out from him where the finish was. It turned out to be a pub at Hough on the Hill and I decided I would aim to end up there.

Looking across the car to the passenger seat I spotted a pretty girl sitting there and noticed that she had one leg encased in plaster. I thought to myself 'there is one I could probably catch even at my advanced age!' She and I got further acquainted at the pub and there started a relationship that ended up in marriage on 22 May 1965.

Cranwell 1963 Dick Turpin's Ride North

After flying one evening at RAF College Cranwell, a colleague and I made our way to our favourite local pub which took us along Ermine Street, the old Roman road from London to Lincoln. On the way back we stopped at a well-known and excellent fish and chip shop. In the village of Ancaster, were a number of locals talking about having seen Dick Turpin riding up the road on his horse. My colleague and I looked at each other tapping our heads as if to motion that they had all lost their senses. We then got into our car to drive north. After a short while we came up behind a man on a horse with a man on a bicycle riding beside him. The horse rider was very well-equipped and wearing a tricorn hat. Tied to each of his boots was a torch with a red lens facing backwards. We could not resist stopping. I called to the man on the horse, 'What are you doing then?' to which he replied 'I am recreating Dick Turpin's ride to York through the night.' Then I said to the man on the bicycle 'What are you doing then?' He said 'I'm from the RSPCA mate. I am here to make sure that he doesn't mistreat the horse!' It is one thing to try to recreate the famous 200 mile trip from London to York on horseback, surely quite another by bicycle! Fortunately, for our sense of our own sanity there was an item in the local newspaper that weekend describing the fact that Dick Turpin's ride had, in fact, been re-enacted during the week. See Appendix A.

While at Cranwell I discovered there were three spare seats available on an indulgence basis on a Britannia aircraft taking exchange cadets to the USAF Academy at Colorado Springs. Anyone occupying these spare seats would not be part of the official visit and might be offloaded as necessary at any time and have to find his own way home.

I managed to encourage two colleagues to come with me and the three of us flew out to Colorado Springs with the cadets. Since we were not part of the official visit we had a lot of time to spare and we hired a car locally with the intention of driving up to the top of Pike's Peak at a height of about 14,000 ft. Unfortunately the top was closed because it was still in snow but we reached a stop at about 9,000 ft, by which time the car was getting a bit breathless. There was a little gift shop attached to the filling station and I wandered around it looking for some small present to take home. I spotted an earthenware ashtray which was labelled 'pine-scented' I picked it up and sure enough a very pleasant pine scent was emitted from the bottom. By way of a joke I asked the girl behind the counter how long the scent would last. She said 'that'll last forever Sir, that's sealed in!' Rather than get involved in a scientific discussion about sealed in perfumes I paid a couple of dollars and bought it. Sure enough within a couple of months the scent had disappeared.

The remainder of the visit was uneventful and we arrived back at Cranwell, not having been offloaded, in good order. The next time I visited the USAF Academy at Colorado Springs was destined to be during my last tour in the RAF when as Deputy Commandant at Cranwell I led a team of cadets on a similar exchange visit, more of which later.

I was lucky to be promoted to Flight Commander fairly soon after joining Cranwell and for a year had the fun job of flying as number three in the four-plane Cranwell Formation Aerobatic Display Team flying Vampires. After a few months flying as number three I was promoted to lead the team for the next season, unfortunately during the current season the station formation aerobatic team at Syerston had had an accident where the number three had collided with the number four both aircraft being lost.

The brilliant solution to that accident, and to ensure that it never happened again, was to reduce all the teams in the Command to a maximum number of three aircraft. So I flew a season as leader of a Cranwell team of three Vampires which was great fun and we did a number of displays at home and at nearby airfields to mark the Battle of Britain in September 1961.

Thinking about it with hindsight I believe that the secret to successful formation acrobatics is to perform manoeuvres that look dangerous to spectators but are in fact quite safe, and have been practised successfully many times. To this end I happened to catch a clip on TV of an American formation aerobatic team which had devised and displayed a formation finale aerobatic manoeuvre called 'Thread the Needle'. I had never heard of this before but I thought it would create a suitable finale for our team of Vampires. The manoeuvre consists of all the aircraft in the team coming in from different directions and crossing at a point in front of the spectators, so appearing to be on a collision course. They have of course to be separated safely. In our case it was done laterally and in terms of height above the ground. I believe that we were the first team to display such a manoeuvre in the UK. It seems to have been appreciated as the letter at Appendix B from a station commander where we performed the 'Thread the Needle' finale manoeuvre states. No discussion on formation aerobatics is complete without mention of my highly skilled and determined wing men, Flight

Lieutenants Paul Crooks and Bob Newell. In a Vampire T11 formation team the most difficult position is number 3 because the T11 was always flown solo from the left hand seat so that in formation the number 3 would be looking across through the empty right hand seat. Our team was the last to fly the Vampire, being succeeded by the Jet Provost.

As well as leading the station formation team I was nominated to fly solo aerobatic displays in the Vampire T11. These too seemed to be appreciated as the letter at Appendix C indicates.

Towards the end of my three-year tour at Cranwell a posting notice arrived. I was posted with acting rank of squadron leader to be the RAF representative at the US Airforce Academy in Colorado Springs. This, I avoided because my recent application for test pilot training took priority. In retrospect my time at Cranwell was demanding and stimulating and I was sorry to leave.

6

Farnborough ETPS

Test pilot training started at Farnborough in the beginning of 1962. I have to admit that I found the syllabus at ETPS (The Empire Test Pilots School) frustratingly out-of-date and for that reason failed to really put my back into it. Another reason was that historical precedent showed that the top boy on each course was sent to Aero Flight at RAE Bedford whereas I desperately wanted to go to the Aeroplane and Armaments Experimental Establishment (A&AEE) at Boscombe Down because of the type of work that would be likely to be involved in. Other reasons were that at the time I was heavily courting Jackie Edwards in Lincolnshire and so spent many hours on the old A1 Great North Road; also another reason was that if we had any spare time in the daylight one was usually able to scrounge a couple of hours continuation training in one of the ETPS fleet of Hunter F4s. The latter tended to take priority for me over bookwork, report writing etc.

Some of the highlights of the course were visits to some of the companies in the Aerospace business, the hospitality was often fairly convivial and it was a good thing that the Viscount in which we travelled was crewed next day by the tutors rather than the students!

Another benefit was having a week off for the Farnborough Air Show which in those days took place in September. In Farnborough week the

ETPS mess tended to fill up with aged Test Pilots whose experiences were interesting and often instructive.

The ETPS aircraft fleet at the time was disappointingly prosaic. It had in previous years included a Fairey Gannet but this was withdrawn because of the habit of students landing with the parking brake on. I felt that the fleet lacked an aircraft with a large powerful piston engine such as the Balliol or Sea Fury.

The course syllabus included a certain amount of gliding which was carried out at weekends. I was lucky in that having delayed my gliding until late in the course I chose a weekend when the air was full of thermals. Every parade ground in Aldershot had a bubble of rising air and I was able to complete my statutory five hours in one sortie! This was not to the amusement of the tutors or other students waiting for a flight in the same aircraft!

Half way through the course I was promoted to squadron leader and also received a QCVSA (Queens Commendation for Valuable Service in the Air) the latter presumably to do with my activities at Cranwell. The promotion had an effect on my posting at the end of the course. One other student had also been promoted and there were two squadron leader slots available, one was to stay at Farnborough and the other was to go to Boscombe Down. I naturally lobbied to be given the Boscombe Down posting which eventually transpired.

Overall 1962 ETPS course was fairly accurately described by one student as 'a 6 month course crammed into a year' Nonetheless enjoyable and instructive!

I arrived at Boscombe Down as a brand new test pilot at the end of 1962, the beginning of a long cold spell which did not break until the March. I did not fly for about three months because the runways were full of snow and ice. We did eventually fly in early March when the thaw came, and by that time I was aching to get in the air again.

After a few weeks in Boscombe Down I was called for my arrival interview with the commandant, Air Commodore Jack Roulston, a South African, a hard man but a great sportsman and aviator. When I entered his office he was reading through a sheaf of papers, presumably my past reports after a while he looked up at me and said 'crikey' or words to that affect; 'you are just like your predecessor a bloody good rugby player but bone idle!'

I was not too impressed by this interview, nor was my predecessor when I related it to him. Despite this start I had a great relationship with the commandant in no small part because of our common interest in game shooting.

On arrival at Boscombe I found I was posted to Support Squadron, not a true test squadron, but they did odd trials that were below the dignity of the other squadrons and also flew support for flight tests at other locations many of them overseas. The squadron had a number of Hastings, a Beverley, an Argosy, a Bristol Freighter, a Valetta and an Anson; all of which I happily converted on to.

After a while it became clear that many of the new aircraft coming to Boscombe were transport types and Support Squadron converted to E Squadron to look after these new types such as the Andover and the Beagle Basset. I became senior pilot of the squadron.

Auto-landing Trials

As I had flown quite a lot of hours in the Argosy it fell to me to take on part of the early work with an automatic landing system produced by Smiths Industries. The system was only single channel so could not be used operationally because it did not have the necessary fail-safe features of a multi-channel system. I must have conducted about 100 test landings with this system, all obviously in good weather conditions and, in fact, it worked surprisingly well.

As the safety pilot, in effect, I kept a close eye on what the auto-landing system was doing so that, in case of a dangerous situation developing I could disconnect at any time by pressing a button and resuming manual flight.

In early trials I was inclined to lose my nerve. I would sit there and see that we were coming down towards the runway and I would wait for the automatic system to do something. I would think 'This is going to fly me right into the ground if I don't do anything' so click! I would disconnect the system because I believed that it was not starting the round out as early as my instincts told me it should have been.

The Smiths engineer who flew with me on the tests got increasingly frustrated as flight after flight I took over. 'It was doing it!' he would say. As far as he was concerned it was a wasted flight. He would be proved right when we got on the ground and saw the records and examination of all the instrumentation showed that my fears were groundless and, in fact, the system had been initiating a round out only a matter of seconds before I had taken control. So the system was testing me, rather than the other way around!

The trials were interesting and I developed quite a degree of faith in the system and would, if necessary, have been prepared to trust it to land me safely. This single-channel system never went into production because it would not have been saleable to airlines for example. Nevertheless, technologies from this system were later incorporated into the multi-channel system. For example, the ability to kick off drift for a cross-wind landing. This was quite clever; the aircraft would have a magnetic compass which would tell it where it was compared to the

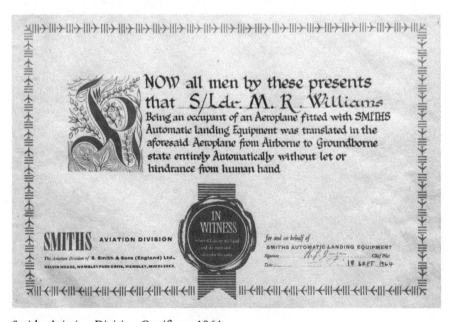

Smiths Aviation Division Certificate 1964.

runway's magnetic heading that had already been fed into it. As you came into the round out the two would be compared and the difference removed by the autopilot.

> Note: A round out is the point at which you pull back on the stick to reduce your rate of descent (also called a flare). The height of the aircraft at which it decided where to do the round out was determined in the test aircraft by a radio altimeter pointed at the ground which told the system accurately how high the aircraft actually was.

I also did some of the early test flying on the Basset, a Beagle Aircraft which was being trialled for the purpose of ferrying V Bomber crews around the UK.

The Basset suffered from some technical teething troubles such as the propeller tips hitting the ground while taxiing. The manufacturers doubted the authenticity of our experiences but eventually solved the problem by a mixture of adjusting the tyre and oleo pressures and cutting bits off the propeller tips.

7

Loss of my Eye

One day in December 1963 I was invited to shoot with a local farmer and all went well until near the end of the day when the guns surrounded a strip of kale. Tom Moore, who coincidentally worked as a clerk in the Officers mess at Boscombe Down, and I stood opposite each other at the end of the strip. As the beaters advanced a cock pheasant took off and flew between Tom and me. As it approached the end of the strip of kale, it is reported that someone shouted don't shoot Tom or you will hit the squadron leader although I did not hear it. Tom fired at the bird and one pellet hit me in the centre of my right eye. In those days very few people had any insurance either against personal injury or third party claims.

Inevitably the RAF held a board of inquiry into the incident and Tom Moore reckoned that the pellet which hit me must have been a ricochet and not a direct hit; this I doubted because I do not recall anything between us from which it might have ricocheted. In fact X-rays show that the offending pellet has flattened on one side which suggests that it either hit something and ricocheted or it was one of the outside pellets in the pattern coming out of the gun.

I drove myself back to Boscombe Down and reported to the medical centre. A car was quickly provided to drive me to Halton RAF Hospital, which, it was reckoned, was the best place to deal with this sort of injury.

I was admitted to the hospital and was gratified and amused to find a present at the side of my bed. It turned out to be a bottle of Scotch whisky sent by a man called Ben Gunn a test pilot for manufacturer Boulton Paul who had been doing some test flying from Boscombe Down in previous weeks. I still, to this day, remember his call sign, which was 'Husky One'.

Examination of my eye by doctors revealed that the damage was probably irreparable as I had already lost all sight in it at that point. It was suggested that the damaged eye should be left in place if only for cosmetic reasons, I agreed, and this was done. In order to prevent infection in the eye it was injected with a liquid from a hypodermic needle once a day. After two weeks doctors told me that they feared that any infection that took hold in the damaged eye could spread to the good eye, presumably via the optic nerve. They suggested that the bad eye was removed to prevent infecting the good eye. This I happily agreed to, particularly since the injections into the damaged eyeball were extremely painful.

My distraught Mother had moved into a hotel in nearby Chesham and spent most of every day with me which was very kind and reassuring but probably overkill in light of the severity of my injury. Squadron Leader Robbie Robinson came to visit and told me that he had been appointed as Senior Pilot on E Squadron at Boscombe Down instead of me, we both felt this was somewhat premature as was proved later. I was fortunate to enjoy a steady stream of visitors as Boscombe Down and Halton were not too far apart and civilian friends called in when they could.

My damaged eye was removed on Christmas Eve 1963 but the offending pellet was left in position embedded in inert tissue behind the eye-socket as it was no threat where it was and to remove it was unnecessary. After another month or so in hospital I was released and returned to Boscombe Down. Once back at Boscombe Down I was naturally anxious to resume flying as soon as possible and I was granted a temporary medical category which allowed me to fly but not solo and not in formation. In addition each pilot who flew with me had to write a report on my flying. These reports would be collated and reviewed when I was given a final long term medical category. I flew as many sorties as I could with as many different pilots as I could in as many different types of aircraft as possible and found no difficulty because of the loss of my eye. The most obvious problem was a large blind spot on my right hand side, but this was more apparent in activities other than flying, such as walking about the streets or driving a car.

I was eventually boarded for a final long term flying category and arrived at the appropriate hour at the Central Medical Establishment in London to be interviewed by an Air Commodore doctor, who, unusually for MOD was wearing uniform and I noted pilot's wings, so I hoped he might be more sympathetic. Eventually after some questioning he signed me off with an A1 category.

Many years later I was at a reception at the then RAF Hospital, Wroughton and spotted a familiar face across the room; it turned out to be the Air Commodore in question, by then long retired. I introduced myself and told him how eternally grateful I was to him; he said 'My God, it's you! Have you ever had an accident?' I said 'No and I am not likely to now as I am doing very little flying'. He said 'I didn't sleep for some time after giving you your A1; I never should have done it!' After repeating my thanks we parted and I left him looking obviously relieved.

I returned happily to Boscombe Down to the consternation of the S of F; and Robbie Robinson and I happily continued in dual harness as Senior Pilots on E Squadron.

With the benefit of hindsight it seems to me that I could not have been in a better place than Boscombe Down when I lost my eye. Boscombe Down had previous experience of two monocular test pilots, 'Cyclops' Brown and Sid Ubee.

Cyclops lost his eye as a result of enemy action when he was attacking a Dornier Bomber in his Spitfire in the Second World War. The rear gunner in the Dornier shattered his windscreen and a piece of it entered Cyclops right eye. He managed to land safely back at his base but the surgeons could not save his eye. He got back to operational flying and eventually became a test pilot at Boscombe Down and attended No.

5 course at the Empire Test Pilots School before becoming Station Commander at Waddington. Cyclop's obituary in the *Daily Telegraph* archives is well worth reading for more amazing details of his life

   Sid Ubee was Commandant of ETPS in 1947/48 but I can find no details of his movements after this but he also had a distinguished career and eventually commanded No. 2 Group with the rank of Air Vice Marshal.

8

Boscombe Down Continued

E Squadron also still had the support role for Boscombe Down and the Argosy was used to transport freight overseas consisting of materials needed for trials by other Boscombe Down aircraft perhaps in different climates. The Argosy was fitted with Rolls Royce Dart turboprop engines which, while being very good, did occasionally give trouble and if this occurred overseas a replacement engine would have to be flown out because Dart engines were not kept stored around the world ready for use.

Consideration concluded that this was not very economical. It was conjectured whether the Argosy could be flown home on three engines if one engine was unserviceable. Obviously the first thing it would have to do on three engines was to take off. This was possible on three working engines if it was run up to full power it could take off climb and cruise successfully. This worked well on the long Boscombe Down runway and in temperate conditions. But as some of our trials took place in tropical areas tests were needed at high temperature.

So in August 1964 I flew the Argosy out to Libya for hot weather three-engine take-off trials. At that time Boscombe Down had a small hot weather trials unit at an airfield in Libya called Idris, an old wartime airfield previously called Castle Benito. The trouble was that its runway was too short to be suitable for the trial. Fortunately there was a nearby airfield called Wheelus, operated by the United States Air Force (USAF) near to Tripoli so we did our trials on their much longer runway, courtesy of the USAF. It all worked out well and three engine take-offs were accepted as a working possibility for the future. The trial was interesting and unusual and provided a very pleasant stay at Idris whilst we did the work at Wheelus. Idris was a pleasant place with a well-equipped Officers' Mess with its own small outdoor swimming pool and the one week stay there made a good break from the probable weather in UK (it was August).

The trip out to Idris in Libya

The flight to Idris and back was interesting and pleasant, being flown mostly within sight of the ground and partly in the hands of Italian Air Traffic Control. Flying over the desert I found fascinating, which experience was to be repeated later in flights over the Empty Quarter in Arabia during my posting to Aden of which more later. It was not uncommon to see pedestrians in the desert, sometimes alone, or accompanied by the odd camel. Many of them seemed to be female incongruously dressed in black, there often appeared to be nowhere particular they had come from or were going to.

About the Beverley at Boscombe Down

I used to fly the Beverley quite a lot, with that and the Argosy parachute drops either at the instrumented range at Larkhill or on Everleigh dropping zone which was not far away; we experimented with various different loads and parachute combinations, and most of our drops were from around 1,500 feet above ground. Eventually some clever clogs decided that it was not a good idea to penetrate enemy territory at that sort of height because one would be in the missile engagement zone for the man-powered Manned Portable Air Defences of which the potential enemy had a lot. It was decided therefore that a system should be developed whereby the load could be dropped from a much lower height. Two rival systems were developed along these lines. The first was at Boscombe Down and the principle was similar to the arresting gear on an aircraft carrier. There would be a cable stretched across the ground attached at either end to a large paddle that was fitted into a circular drum full of water. The hook in the Beverley was designed to catch this arresting cable it would pull a platform out of the aircraft to land on its shock absorbed bottom on the ground and slide to a safe stop. This worked well generally but the snag was that people had to be on the ground first to set up the whole system not least digging in two big drums. This was a major disadvantage. The rival system, Ultra Low Level Approach (hence ULLA) developed at Farnborough, was to fly in suitably low, deploy a load which would be pulled out by a small parachute. Both systems worked quite well so the decision came to a bit of a shoot-out which involved exercise Unison at Cranwell. Both Beverley's took part and there were numerous rehearsals. All rehearsals were in good weather and there were no problems delivering either system. Unfortunately the weather on the actual day was very murky and we had to perform a long run in. We were not aligned with the necessary track over the arresting cable early enough, so we did not pick it up. On the other hand the Farnborough Beverly did shed its load successfully so was therefore selected for development. The ultra-low level delivery was fun to fly and we did, in practice successfully deliver many loads. The loads would be on a cushioned platform and were made up of suitably weighted items. A popular load was compo-rations which came in tins. Occasionally the load would break loose from the platform and the tins would be dispensed in a shower of shining metal, at which point cars would converge on the site from all over the airfield driven by people who had been watching the action and hoping for a platform break up and free delivery of compo rations. Apart from the need to set up the arrester gear the other disadvantage of the Boscombe system was that you needed to fly pretty low for the hook to catch the arresting cable and it was possible that the main wheels would touch the ground before you got to it. This meant that you had to have a nice smooth run in in case you touched the main wheels on the ground. This would clearly be an operational disadvantage.

Some drops in the Argosy could be quite exciting. Some loads such as one tonne containers were allowed to run out of the fuselage and over the lip by gravity because at that speed the aircraft dropped floor would be sufficiently inclined that the containers would roll back on their own. This would cause a massive shift in the centre of gravity and we got to the stage a few times where the elevator was on the forward stop for about eight seconds whilst the load rolled back down the fuselage altering the centre of gravity. One hoped at that stage that no problems would occur, such as an engine failure. The burly loadmaster down below was usually able to assist gravity adequately.

The odd diversion—amusing in its way—used to occur during my early years at Boscombe Down. Occasionally one of the large aircraft, I think it was a Vulcan, was refuelled on the hard standing outside the E Squadron hangar.

If the internal fuel tanks were filled in the wrong order the centre of gravity could move far enough back for the aircraft to tilt over and sit back on its tail. This made the aircraft difficult to move again and caused considerable embarrassment to those involved. Fortunately, the solution was easy: to amend the order in which the tanks were filled so that such occurrences were not frequent.

One evening in the bar of the mess I got to talking to Squadron Leader Mike Adams, later Air Vice Marshal, but then a test pilot on A Squadron at Boscombe Down.

He had his left arm in plaster because of a wrist injury sustained as a result of contact with the wall of the squash court. He commented that he wanted to go to RAE Bedford for a meeting but was not allowed to fly solo because of the injury to his 'throttle arm'. I said: 'Well I am not allowed to fly solo either and I want to go to Bedford to talk about auto landing. So why do we not go together in the Meteor 7. I could work the throttles and you could do the look out.' This we eventually agreed to do, on the day in question we flew uneventfully to Bedford and taxied into dispersal after which a civilian ground crewman came to help us unstrap. At the time I had not yet got an artificial eye so was wearing a black patch. The ground crewman looked us over and said 'blimey sirs, what's this then? The Battle of Britain!' We both had successful meetings and flew uneventfully back to Boscombe Down where no questions were asked.

In order to try to repair some of the binocular vision I had lost I took to playing squash in the courts nearby. One evening, and perhaps because of a rapid head movement, my artificial eye popped out and rolled across the floor. My opponent immediately and unkindly accused me of unsporting gamesmanship. I replied that had I worn a black patch instead of or over the bad eye he would still have accused me of gamesmanship. The loss of the eye had not really affected my previously poor standard of play, although it has to be said that the odd 'air shot' did occur. By way of compensation, I got more exercise running about than I had previous to the loss of the eye.

In September 1965 I supported a trial with an Argosy of a Royal Naval Buccaneer in the United States. We visited Patuxent River, the US Naval Test Centre and later Edwards Air Force base, the US Air Force test centre.

During our time staying in the visiting officers' quarters at Patuxent we were befriended by a local newspaper man who was kind enough to lend us a car. This was generous and something of a surprise when the car turned out to be a Pontiac GTO, very much a hot rod in those days. The experience of sitting at traffic lights in this left hand drive monster surrounded by drivers whose sole aim was to out-accelerate a GTO was something to be remembered!

While at Edwards I was offered a flight in a Hercules C130H which I accepted with alacrity because at the time I was convinced the RAF should be buying the Hercules. I was allowed to fly the Hercules on a trip from Edwards to Travis US air force base and back and afterwards wrote a report on my findings (see Appendix D) which I fed into the system at Boscombe Down. I was very grateful to the captain for allowing me to do more of the flying than I had any right to expect.

Eventually the RAF did buy the Hercules and very useful it has been; I would like to think that my report had a small part in this decision.

Towards the end of my time at Boscombe I became the lead test pilot for the acceptance trials of the Andover military freighter. This was basically a Hawker Siddeley 748 which had been modified for rear loading of freight—vehicles etc. In order for the freight ramp to reach the ground the undercarriage had been modified to kneel hydraulically. The necessity to fit a kneeling undercarriage rather negated the benefits of buying a low wing aircraft rather than a high wing aircraft such as the Handley Page Dart or Herald.

One interesting feature of flying at Boscombe Down was the opportunity to fly one of the three Harvards on strength; these were used for photo chase with a photographer in the rear seat. The Harvard had a wide speed range given its retractable undercarriage which made it ideal for this job. It was quite a handful on the ground, especially in a cross wind given its narrow track undercarriage. Many unplanned ground loops were performed on the wide main runway at Boscombe by pilots who had no previous experience of tailwheel aircraft.

During my time at Boscombe Down Jackie and I got married in her home village of Ruskington and after a honeymoon in Scotland we rented Till Cottage in Winterbourne Stoke as our first home. Till was a charming two-up, two-down thatched cottage with a garden running down to the river Till. It had its own water supply pumped from a well under the kitchen floor up to a holding tank in the roof. The pump was activated by the water level dropping below a set level, this was a problem because the pump was extremely noisy and so overnight guests had to be told not to flush the lavatory during the night as it would wake the whole house!

The cottage had the customary low-beamed ceilings and to avoid bumping my head every few paces I had to stoop. One day in the Boscombe Down ante-room after lunch I heard a comment 'look at poor old Mike, all bent over and he has only been married a few weeks.'

Occasionally visitors, often Americans, would arrive to look at the 'pretty thatched cottage' and we would show them round. They had usually done the Olde English Tour and on one occasion one lady was heard to remark 'Gee Elmer, we have seen Anne Hathaway's cottage, but there are people actually living here.'

9

Aden

When the time grew near for the end of my test pilot's tour at Boscombe Down I started to try to negotiate an extension; mainly in order to complete the acceptance trials of the Andover MF (Military Freighter), for which I was project pilot. I was not successful and eventually my posting notice arrived. It was to Headquarters Middle East Command in Aden as Command Flight Safety Officer (CFSO).

I was to replace Squadron Leader Ted Mellor, another test pilot who had been a tutor at ETPS when I did the course in Farnborough in 1962. It appeared that Middle East Command valued having a test pilot as CFSO because of the number of different aircraft types that were operated in the Command. I was not over-enthused because it was basically a ground job although I might be able to scrounge a ride in the Command Hunters occasionally.

At that time the City of Aden was part of the Federation of South Arabia which had been set up by Britain (the colonial power) to prepare for the handover of power on independence.

The Aden Emergency which had started in 1963 was ongoing and riots in Crater in 1966 exacerbated the situation so I arrived at a fairly difficult time and the areas we could visit were considerably curtailed.

Partly because the service families who had lived in Crater had to be rehoused elsewhere there were no married quarters immediately available in Aden so I went out alone at first and stayed in the officers' mess Tarshyne; a comfortable air-conditioned place with a private beach with a shark-netted swimming area; while I awaited allocation of a married quarter so that Jackie could come and join me. Eventually we were allocated a quarter, a small flat in a fairly old block in Maala and Jackie flew out. In the absence of Jackie I had to take over the inventory of the married quarter, signing for the crockery etc. Jackie duly arrived and we lived happily in the quarter for a while, but after a couple of months we were allocated another quarter in a new block of flats in Maala.

This involved a march out from the first quarter, which I undertook because I had done the march in. In due course a representative of the Barrack Warden's empire arrived to do the march out. It is never the same person who does the march out as the march in, this being a matter of principle.

We went through the inventory with the barrack warden calling out the items from the list, which I held up for inspection.

We moved on steadily until we came to the item: *Dishes, Butter, (Officers)*.

I pushed forward the butter dish I had signed for on the march in. He said: 'That is *Dishes, Butter, (Airmen)*.'

'What is the difference?' I asked.

'About 16 and nine pence' he said.

I was baffled, I told him that I had taken over the butter dish in good faith and he would not be getting a penny from me. He made no comment so presumably accepted the explanation.

When we came to march into the new quarter Jackie kindly undertook to do the inventory check etc.

The flat was in a new high-rise block just off the Maala straight; originally called Churchill Block, but subsequently named Al Faaiz. Given the security situation all the servicemen living in the married quarter blocks in the town took turns to mount guard at the entrance to the quarters armed with a service revolver in order to deter any action by FLOSY (the front for the Liberation of South Yemen) which was one of several dissident groups. Although there were many areas which were classed as out of bounds, such as Crater, families enjoyed freedom to shop, visit the beach and eat out, although a curfew was eventually imposed and all service personnel and dependants had to be off the streets between 10 p.m. and 6 a.m. By this time I had developed such a tan that I would get stopped at road blocks being mistaken for an Arab.

Life for the families in Aden was quite restricted at that time as there were few places other than the main street and the beach that they could go, also there were quite often curfews called which meant everyone staying in their flats until the all clear. Jackie was pleased to be offered a job with one of the then Aden Government departments and gladly accepted. She worked Arab hours, having Friday off and working Sundays, as everyone worked a long morning and had the rest of the day off this was not too restrictive on our time together. She also got paid in local currency and paid local tax, considerably less than I was liable for!

At one stage a shark managed to get into the netted area off the beach at Tarshyne which therefore had to be closed to swimmers. The Navy sprang into action releasing three depth charges in the enclosed area to kill or drive the shark out. Unfortunately only two of the charges exploded and the other one did not kill the shark so the beach had to remain closed for another week whilst the unexploded charge was recovered!

The job as CFSO was interesting because flight safety in an operational environment—which Aden was at the time—involved compromise. The Hunters used to be sent up country to do low-level flag waves over hostile positions often resulting in them coming home with holes in them from small arms fire. This was clearly a flight safety hazard in that one day small arms damage might prove sufficient to disable the aircraft. I consequently felt bound to advise the operators that I did not think it was a good thing to fly at low level over dissident positions. I was politely told that operations were their business and flight safety was mine, and the flag waves continued.

As CFSO I reported directly to the Senior Air Staff Officer (SASO) who at the time was one Air Commodore Freddie Sowrey. Sowrey was a pilot and had commanded a squadron of Javelins in the UK at one time, so I think we were both instinctively on the same wavelength. As CFSO my job was flight safety publicity as well as reporting and investigating incidents and accidents. As part of the flight safety publicity one task was to produce a quarterly flight safety magazine called *Desert Wings*, for which I produced the material but which had to be printed by the Command Printing Unit. The Command Printing Unit was a joint operation and they had to set priorities. *Desert Wings* took lower priority than printing rules of engagement yellow cards for the troops. The result was that I regularly came under pressure from SASO as *Desert Wings* approached its next deadline. I was unable to give it any priority with the Command Printing Unit so it was often late coming out which was unfortunate but as I saw it inevitable.

We were fortunate in not having any serious accidents. Resident aircraft on the airfield at Khormaksar were restricted to two squadrons of Hunters 8 and 43 and 34 Squadron of Shackletons. There were also Twin Pioneers and Argosys plus Wessex Helicopters. I managed to get trips in the latter two and also managed a trip flying a Hunter 7 for an hour courtesy of the various squadrons. There were also two more Hunter squadrons at the airfield of RAF Muharraq at Bahrain, which also came under the aegis of Middle East Command. Different transport aircraft staged through as Aden was still a very important staging post to the Gulf and farther east.

The tour was interesting in that I had occasion once or twice to travel up country and on one occasion undertook a visit to Majunga an airfield on the island of Madagascar where for a while the RAF had a Shackleton squadron to help enforce the blockade of Rhodesia (now Zimbabwe). The blockade, also known as the Beira Patrol, was in response to the Rhodesian government's Unilateral Declaration of Independence (UDI) in November 1965 following a disagreement over the independence settlement with Britain, the colonial power.

I also had responsibility for flight safety in the Sultan of Oman's Air force where there were always a number of RAF pilots on exchange.

One of the joys of being in the Headquarters with a roving commission was the ability to get up country from time to time and

A favorite cover of Desert Wings Flight Safety Magazine, a Beverley landing in the Radfan, June 1967.

visit some of the small outposts that we maintained there. This was sometimes courtesy of the Twin Pioneers and sometimes the Army Air Corps who kept both rotary and fixed wing aircraft in theatre. I particularly remember flying with Wing Commander Eddie Rigg in the Argosy to such places as Salalah, Sharjah and Muharraq.

The climate in Aden was basically hot and dry although humidity could be uncomfortable at times. Rain was almost unheard of, and at the time we were there it was said there had been no serious rain for fifty years.

On the day the United Nations' peacekeeping delegation flew in on a visit to Aden, the skies opened. It rained about six inches in eight hours. This resulted in widespread flooding in the streets, which because it 'never' rained had grown up with no drains. The water, running down off the mountains, could not escape out into the sea so the roads became rivers. The Aden taxi drivers, who had never seen floodwater before, worked on the principle that the quicker one got through it the better. They pointed their taxis at the standing water and accelerated. We stood on our balcony and watched taxi after taxi drive into the water get flooded, and stop. The result was that the streets were littered with flooded taxis for a week or so. Some of the flood water was eventually released into the sea by the Army who drove a tank through the sea wall.

The rest was left to dry out, resulting in considerable debris, including dead goats and some of the shacks that had been washed down off the mountain. The mud left behind eventually dried out and blew away as dust in the wind, which was unpleasant.

The hills which had been barren bare rock exploded into colour from some of the seeds that had probably been dormant for nearly fifty years.

One of the perks for families living in Aden at the time was that once a year they were allowed a free air flight to Kenya either, at their choice, to Mombasa on the coast or to Nairobi. Jackie and I made use of this offer opting to go to Nairobi rather than Mombasa in that we saw plenty of the beach in Aden without needing to go and lie on the beach at Mombasa. We stayed at the Norfolk Hotel in Nairobi and after a couple of days hired a car and took off into the foothills of Mount Kenya. We soon discovered an Inn called the Izaak Walton Inn which had trout fishing on the river Rupingazi nearby.

The Rupingazi had a stock of rainbow trout which the local expert declared could only be caught on a trout fly known as a 'coachman'. I inwardly rejected this advice thinking, rather arrogantly that rainbow trout would probably take the same sort of fly the world over and therefore those in Kenya would take the same flies as those used in the UK successfully. The form for a day's fishing was that one would be accompanied by a young African man as a ghillie or guide. The ghillie was paid half a crown in old money and one was strictly advised that under no circumstances should this be exceeded because it would spoil the market by increasing their expectations. The ghillies were sparsely dressed and washed irregularly so the advised form was to choose a ghillie from a line by walking along the line downwind and choosing the least ripe because he would have to be driven in the car to the fishing, preferably with all the windows open.

The ghillies proved to be highly skilled and invaluable; if one's fly caught in a tree the ghillie was up the tree in a flash to dislodge it, and if one caught a fish the ghillie was instantly in the water with a net to fetch it out. Well worth half a crown a day.

After fishing for some time without success with various flies such as those used to catch rainbows in the UK I reluctantly tied on a coachman which resulted in immediate success. Sure enough, the Kenyan rainbow trout only wanted coachman flies.

Rather more interesting from a fishing point of view was a day in boat on Lake Naivasha after fresh water bass. Pretty regular bites but no huge success.

We felt obliged while in Kenya to spend a few nights at the famous Outspan Hotel and indulge in low level safari, using my new Pentax Spotmatic camera recently purchased for a few East African Shillings, the then Aden Currency.

We hired a guide with a car who managed to show us a great variety of the wonderful wildlife in the Aberdare National Park; cheetahs, hippos, giraffes, lions and so on, in fact almost everything except elephants. We did another short trip into the Nairobi National Park when we returned to the capital but still no elephants.

We had flown out from Aden in a Comet to Eastleigh but returned in an Argosy because the Comet was not available, a considerable difference in the comfort on the return journey, but the price was right!

As a result of the deteriorating security situation and the imminent withdrawal of British forces, families were evacuated from Aden during the first half of 1967 before the final British withdrawal in November of that year. Jackie flew home by VC10 leaving me behind in the Tarshyne officers' mess.

The flight safety empire in Aden was to move up to Bahrain when Aden was evacuated in 1967 and although my last few weeks in Aden were busy organising the move, I was eagerly awaiting my posting notice. When it arrived it was something of a shock, to do something that I had in no way anticipated. I was to command the university air squadron in Oxford. OUAS would normally have been commanded by a graduate of that University, presumably the RAF was unable to find an MA (Oxon) at the time and so had to make do with me, a graduate MA (Trinity College Dublin) no doubt with Oxford's agreement.

With the job came acting rank of wing commander. At the time the squadron was based at RAF Bicester just north of Oxford, where its fleet of De Havilland Chipmunks was kept and its flying took place from the on-site grass airfield. The posting was completely unexpected, but a flying job with acting rank was not to be sneezed at and I left Aden a happy man, though I think somewhat to the surprise of SASO.

10

Oxford

Prior to taking up the appointment of CO of Oxford University Air Squadron (OUAS) I was entitled to a flying refresher course that was to take place at Manby on the Lincolnshire coast in the Jet Provost. The flying refresher passed uneventfully and for the duration we rented a small flat on the seafront in the coastal resort of Sutton on Sea. The flying was pleasant, even if the jet-powered tricycle undercarriage Jet Provost was not entirely relevant to the Chipmunk to come. I did however realise how much my flying ability had deteriorated during my time on the ground in Aden, mainly in the areas of speed of reaction to the radio and instrument scan.

Oxford University Air Squadron was formed in 1925 and trained many who went on to have distinguished careers including two holders of the VC—Leonard Cheshire and Lord Lyell. Other notable ex-members include Julian Amery, and the actors Richard Burton and Robert Hardy. At the time I took over command there were 60 students and 6 flying instructors plus ground and admin staff.

A married quarter at RAF Bicester went with the job of CO at OUAS and we duly moved in out of the Sutton on Sea flat. The other residents of the station at Bicester were an RAF Regiment squadron; they were interesting neighbours even if the RAF regiment junior officers did not always see eye to eye with the OUAS students who used the officers' mess from time to time. No serious events occurred however as common sense eventually supervened on both sides to prevent debates getting too heated.

The air squadron seemed in good heart when I took over from my predecessor Wing Commander Brian Iles who later sadly died as a result of a diving accident in the Mediterranean while he was on leave. I was fortunate in having an excellent chief flying instructor, Squadron Leader George England, to whom incidentally I was to hand over the squadron when I left two years later. George England ran a very tight ship with the flying side and my only lurking nervousness was the thought of 60 OUAS students flying solo around the Bicester area whilst heavy metal in the shape of USAF F111s hurtled down the glide path into nearby Upper Heyford. My fears fortunately proved groundless.

The squadron was also lucky to have a senior member, one Doctor Colin Bailey, a don at Keble College who was invaluable as a source of advice and expertise on the University.

Annual highlights of the UAS year were the summer camps normally undertaken at an operational RAF station where the squadron deployed and flew from for a couple of weeks and students could get the necessary continuity of instruction and flying to make good progress. For our first summer camp in 1968 we were unlucky not to get an operational station as a base, going instead to Tangmere in Sussex, flying from Shoreham just outside Worthing, which was quite adequate from a flying point of view, a large grass airfield, but lacking the RAF presence. We were made very welcome by Beagle Aviation which was based at Shoreham and which produced the Basset Aircraft bought by the RAF and on which I had done some test-flying at Boscombe Down in 1964.

Our second year summer camp in 1969 was at RAF Waddington in Lincolnshire, then the home of V bombers; Vulcans. I wondered to what extent this might inspire my undergraduates to join the RAF, but to my surprise several of them were fired up by the role they had seen at Waddington and we achieved several recruits to the Service later in that year.

It was at a time when UASs were coming under increasing pressure to regard recruiting for the RAF as their primary role. This was something I did my best to resist, because I reasoned that it would, if it became obvious, not foster good relations with the University, upon which we obviously depended entirely for our continued existence, even if only because the old corrugated iron hangar we occupied in Manor Road Oxford as our town headquarters belonged to the University. I also felt strongly that a major part of the role was to foster an appreciation of the importance of air power and aviation among those who might well in later life progress into positions of power in the land. All the university air squadrons were also under pressure to reduce operational costs such as by having fewer students and Oxford was no exception and during my time the numbers were reduced from 60 to 40 members.

In the middle of my time with OUAS I eventually decided to undertake some staff training, something I had been putting off until then on the grounds that it did not involve flying, but by mid-1967 the Service had introduced something called the Individual Studies School, a correspondence course in staff work. This I could no longer logically avoid so I signed up and eventually passed the fairly primitive exams and got a poor man's staff qualification.

The command of the air squadron was a bare two years which was only to be expected, and with hindsight was a happy and successful time during which my acting rank of wing commander was upgraded to be substantive.

I was also offered, and accepted, incorporation into Oxford University. This was offered by the then Vice Chancellor Kenneth Turpin, Provost of Oriel College and included dining rights. To accept my incorporation I was required to present myself at a Commencements Ceremony in the Sheldonian Theatre and when I enquired about the appropriate dress for the occasion I was told RAF uniform, gown and mortar board—so that is what I did. I felt that this was an honour not just for me but for the squadron and the part they play in University life.

Our time at Oxford was also marked by the arrival of our three children; first our son Richard in April 1968 and subsequently twins

Peter and Jane in June 1969. On the domestic side one of the most memorable aspects of the tour was our central heating boiler which burnt coke. The coke was housed in a vertical hopper above the actual fire which from time to time would ignite entirely leading to massive overheating and warning noises from the boiling water and result in the fire section arriving to extinguish it.

At the end of my very happy tour with OUAS inevitably another ground job arrived; to attend a course at the Joint Services Staff College at Latimer in Buckinghamshire. During that course, which was less than six months long, we remained in the married quarter in Bicester and I lived in the mess at Latimer during the week. The course was interesting in that it covered the whole world and included students from all three UK services and from many other countries. At the end of the course our postings came through and mine initially was to stay on at Latimer as the RAF directing staff. This did not appeal to me enormously and perhaps fortunately it was in fact changed because one of the other students who had been posted into a Central Staff Planning Appointment in MOD Whitehall had failed the necessary enhanced security clearance procedure and I was posted in to replace him. While at Latimer I had become a specialist on Burma. This proved entirely irrelevant to my responsibilities in the Central Staff at MOD, which covered the UK participation in National, and NATO, ACE Mobile Force (AMF) and UK Mobile Force (UKMF) exercises.

11

Ministry of Defence

The Central Staff job involved membership of a tri-service team at wing commander level and included an involvement in planning for force levels in Northern Ireland where the troubles were at their peak. In particular I was involved in UK reinforcement in Operation Motorman with a colleague Commander David Aldrich RN. In the middle of the night we had to find a name for the forthcoming operation and on the principle of *eenie, meenie, miney, mo* we selected a word from the dictionary beginning with mo; this seemed as good a way as any to approach the job. The name, Motorman, was accepted as to object would have meant that the objector would have had to find an alternative. The Northern Ireland force level planning was fascinating and involved a visit to the province to discuss matters on the spot.

As part of the Assistant Chief of Defence Staff's planning team I was also responsible for writing the operational plan for the withdrawal of British forces from Malta, which had been demanded by the then Prime Minister, Dom Mintoff, this, happily, involved several visits to the island and eventually the final plan had to be written overnight. My efforts seem to have been generally appreciated, although I had no desire to establish myself as a planning specialist.

I found Central Staff to be challenging because whatever one's view of the correct solution to planning for all three services one was

E.R.

W422/01

D of DOP

Copy to:

VCAS
AUS(D Staff)

COS 1014/5/1/72

    CDS has seen this paper on Malta
and entirely shares (my) view that it is
an excellent piece of work produced at
very high speed in difficult conditions.
Would you please pass this approbation
on to Wing Commander Williams for his major
part in it.

me too —
allthough I may
not have had time to!
say so!

D/DOP

MRS
7/1 F(Air)

7/1

VCDS

6 January 1972

The Survivors in Malta

of

The Winter War
(January to March 1972)

having returned to normal peace-time conditions
(including a near repetition in January 1973 of the events of a year ago)
Send greetings to their former collaborators
on the surprising anniversary of the
signing of the Agreement
26th March 1972
and assure them they are
remembered with affection
(and may be required again at any time)

Survivors of Malta cartoon.

inevitably expected by one's own Service to take the RAF view rather than look at the situation in general and conclude what was right from a joint point of view.

NATO planning was pretty stodgy stuff enlivened by the odd amusing item. One amusement I remember was a semi-serious proposal to form a French/German corps in NATO! Advanced planning for this was bedevilled by the inevitable argument about command arrangements. The British solution was a classic compromise whereby command would be exercised by a German general if the corps were advancing and by a French general if it was retreating this frivolous suggestion was instrumental in causing the idea to be dropped. It amused the Germans but not the French!

NATO planning was by its nature slow moving and staid stuff likened by one disillusioned Brit to trying to swim in porridge.

Adjacent to our offices on the fifth floor of the main Ministry of Defence building in Whitehall was the office of the Chiefs of staff Secretariat (COSSEC) consisting of a tri-service group of mid-rank officers with appropriate security clearance who sat in on the afternoon meetings of the Chiefs of Staff Committee and subsequently drafted the minutes. On the wall of the COSSEC office hung a notice which said:

And so as the great men repair to their dinner
The secretaries stay getting thinner and thinner
Racking their brains to record and report
What the great men will think that they ought to have thought.

I was allocated an Officers' Married Quarter (OMQ) at Whitley Wood, just outside Reading from where I commuted daily by rail via Paddington. Our time in the married quarters there was marked by the building of the M4 motorway which cut across some of the local roads and one of the results was that the OMQ became a short cut from the nearby council estate to a popular pub on the other side of the new motorway. Youths, in a happy state, used to return from the pub late at night via the OMQs, shouting, singing and running sticks along the wooden railings. At the end of a long day in London I was lying in the bath when the noise started and I lost my cool and leapt out of the bath, opened the window in my naked state and shouted 'be quiet or I'll ring the police', out of the darkness came the instant reply 'Get back on the job mate!' I still have not thought of an appropriate response to that!

CTTO

A posting notice duly arrived and we were delighted to be returning to Boscombe Down, unfortunately not in a flying job but as a representative of Central Trials and Tactics Organisation (CTTO) and we eventually moved into a married quarter on the station at Boscombe Down. The task of A&AEE Boscombe Down was to ensure that the aircraft being purchased by the RAF were capable of performing to the standard that was required of them and that the manufacturers said they could and my brief was to monitor the trials on new aircraft entering service such as the Jaguar and ensure that operational factors were fully considered. This remit became well known to A&AEE staff with the result that I was often, jocularly, regarded as an RAF spy. This impression was reinforced by the fact that I was required to report regularly and in person to RAF Strike Command Headquarters at High Wycombe. It became plain that when I entered A&AEE offices the papers on the desks would be immediately turned over thus preventing me from reading them, presumably on the assumption that I had received training in upside-down reading.

The work was not uncongenial and I was, from time to time, able to scrounge the odd flight in various A&AEE aircraft.

Presumably my work was not regarded as particularly important because I was not replaced when posted out after a year.

Little Rissington

After only about a year at Boscombe another posting arrived, to be station commander at RAF Little Rissington in Gloucestershire which housed the fixed wing element of Central Flying School, the Red Arrows and Examining Wing, with the rank of group captain. This displeased the authorities in CTTO to whom I reported but it was good news for me since it included the entire fleet of fixed wing aircraft based at Little Rissington and the Red Arrows based at nearby Kemble. CFS had its own Bulldogs and Jet Provosts which I could fly as required.

As mentioned before the main task of CFS was training flying instructors and this was still the case. Students came from different countries including many Commonwealth members and there was always a United States Air Force pilot instructor on an exchange tour.

The commandant of Central Flying lived at Little Rissington but was also responsible for the rotary wing of CFS which was based at Ternhill. The commandant when I arrived was Air Commodore Roy Crompton whose account of flying with the Red Arrows to North America via Lapland in the short range Gnat was fascinating and he left me very much to my own devices.

Roy Crompton was succeeded by Air Commodore John Severne who in turn left me to get on with my job. It was fortunate that he himself had been a station commander at RAF Kinloss so he felt no need to interfere with what I was doing but would always give support when needed.

My time at Little Rissington was happy and relatively uneventful as far as flying accidents went. At the time we were doing some of the early flying on the Jetstream which suffered a series of unexplained engine run downs. Eventually after long investigation the problem recurred during ground runs and it was discovered that at certain engine RPM a vibration occurred which caused a high pressure fuel cock to partially close. This resulted in an engine shut down. To my mind this was a design fault in that the HP cock should have been designed so that it was locked in the open position.

We occasionally had visits by senior officers from other countries who were thinking of sending us students. I remember one visit by the chief of air staff of the Egyptian Air Force accompanied by a number of staff officers. The latter spent some time running up and down the corridor in the mess looking at the photos of past courses to see which Egyptians they could recognise, none had been on the course since 1956 when relations soured because of the Suez affair. Talking to the Egyptian CAS during lunch I enquired whether he had enjoyed the Farnborough Air Show which I knew he had visited the previous day. That was the day the Lockheed SR71 Blackbird had set a new transatlantic air speed record and I enquired if he had seen it. He replied 'I see them every day over my country.'

While at Little Rissington I was initially in the chain of command for the RAF aerobatic team, the Red Arrows. I took advantage of this to enable me to fly as passenger with each member of the team during a practice display which gave me a good idea of the discipline and the excitement of some of the manoeuvres involved. Although under the command of RAF Little Rissington the Red Arrows flew from RAF Kemble just down the road which gave them an airfield to practice over without disturbance to any other flying activities.

It was a difficult time, because of the global oil crisis, fuel was in short supply and the new Red Arrows leader had been required to practice at 2000 ft above ground level. This restriction severely affected the rate of progress towards display clearance and occasioned a change of leader which fortunately did not interfere significantly with progress to clearance. Mainly as a result of these problems I felt that the chain of command for the Red Arrows was too complicated and at my request I was taken out of the chain.

The RAF felt it should be seen to be economising during this time and therefore reduced the size of the station commander's car from a large Rover to a Mini which arrived complete with the station commander's standard flying from the bonnet.

One of the great honours and pleasures of commanding Little Rissington was that the station enjoyed the freedom of the nearby borough of Cheltenham. The station personnel paraded through the streets once a year and we were all well entertained to refreshments in the Town Hall afterwards. It was sometimes difficult to find enough service men to march through the town as there was a feeling then that drill and marching were properly the preserve of the RAF Regiment, in that respect female members of staff were very helpful as they seemed to have no hang-ups about drill or marching and were excellent at both.

Little Rissington was fortunate in that despite the occasional noise complaint it enjoyed excellent relations with the surrounding area. CFS also had a mascot, a pelican looked after at Birdland in Bourton on the Water then under control of Len Hill. The Pelican, Flight Lieutenant Frederick, used to be wheeled up for dining-in nights and for Royal or VIP visits. We were also very honoured and pleased to have HM the Queen Mother as commandant-in-chief. She used to visit us regularly and the Pelican was always brought up to greet her. He was an evil bird who had a particular liking for the shiny buttons down the front of the dress uniform and was not averse to plucking one off, much to the amusement of the Queen Mother.

CFS was also the parent unit for the Examining Wing (colloquially known as 'the trappers') whose staff visited many different units in the RAF to check on instructional standards and was also fortunate enough to be invited to a number of foreign countries to report on their instructional standards. I myself was fortunate enough to go with 'the trappers' on a visit to the Royal Australian Airforce towards the end of my time as station commander.

Early in 1976 it was decided that it was no longer cost effective to keep Little Rissington open as a flying station purely to house fixed wing CFS. It was therefore decided to close it with effect from the middle of the year and move CFS to Cranwell. At the time the Army was desperately short of accommodation in the UK and a battalion of the Irish Rangers took over the station at Little Rissington.

We left with heavy hearts as 'Rissy' had always been a very happy station.

14

Royal Naval War College, Greenwich

When the station closed in mid-1976 I was posted to be the RAF directing staff at the Royal Naval War College at Greenwich. The main responsibility of the War College was to run the Senior Officers' War Course (SOWC). The SOWC, the Old Soaks Course, as it was popularly known, was a Tri-Service course at Group Captain–Brigadier–Commodore level and in effect was a shortened version of the then prestigious Imperial Defence College (IDC)

I was initially doubtful about this, but in fact, and in retrospect it was interesting and useful. The directing staff on the course consisted of a naval captain, director, called Peter Beeson. There were three other directing staff, one from each of the UK services at group captain level. As RAF directing staff, my task was to organise the air side of the course and conduct the relevant parts of it, which included a number of visits, mainly to UK formations, but sometimes abroad as in Norway, which will be mentioned later. An early lesson I learned was that releasing a group of senior service officers from a coach and getting them back together again was like herding cats!

The SOWC was housed in the prestigious premises of the Royal Naval College Greenwich, where it co-habited with the Royal Navy's staff course. As well as students from the UK's three services, the course also included some students from friendly foreign countries, which while being interesting, did impose certain restrictions as regards security clearances, which inhibited examination and discussion of certain aspects such as those with a NATO or a UK eyes only security classification.

As there were no married quarters available at Greenwich I initially commuted weekly from Little Rissington. It was with some relief therefore that we were eventually offered a married quarter at RAF Biggin Hill, which was a comfortable daily commute by car, through such salubrious areas of South London as Catford. The time that we spent at Biggin Hill proved pleasant and productive, including as it did access to the swimming pool where our three children learned to swim during the heat wave summer of 1976. Our local church on the station was the beautiful Battle of Britain Memorial Chapel and it was happily a regular occurrence to meet ex Battle of Britain pilots visiting the chapel and the officers' mess.

My time at Greenwich included the year of 1977, which was the Queen's Silver Jubilee year, and I recall manning the steps on the river at Greenwich and saluting as the Queen passed by afloat. We were all rewarded with a tot of rum although the regular rum ration had been abolished by the then Chief of Naval Staff Sir Michael Le Fanu who had red hair and therefore became known as 'dry ginger'. Admiral Le Fanu came to give a talk to one of the courses while I was there and on arrival he walked up to the lectern and hung a notice over it which read:

There they go and I must hurry to catch them up for I am their leader.

This set the tone for a very amusing and informative lecture.

One fairly regular attraction was the availability of musical concerts in the chapel by small groups such as The Academy of St Martin in the Fields, then conducted by Neville Marriner. I vividly remember one such concert when they played the Four Seasons by Vivaldi. Despite pessimistic appearances the acoustics in the chapel were brilliant which added much to the pleasure of the occasion. Every working day started with a ten minute service in the chapel for all staff and students, a very civilised way to begin the day. Another attraction of my time at Greenwich was the regular access to the famous Painted Hall which was used as a mess dining room and for functions such as our summer ball.

One of the more memorable visits undertaken during the course was to Norway and since we were to travel by air it fell to me to organise the visit. Happily I discovered at a fairly early stage that it would be cheaper for us to hire an aircraft including the crew to go with us all the way around, rather than to fly by scheduled services. We duly chartered a small aircraft including the crew, with two personable stewardesses to ferry us around the various places that we needed to visit. The itinerary naturally included a penetration into the Arctic Circle, where we were fortunate to be able to see the midnight sun descending to the horizon and then rising again. The company of the stewardesses was much enjoyed, especially by some of the more mature students who were enjoying, even if only temporarily, an absence from the 'trouble and strife'.

15

UKCICC

A happy time at Greenwich was eventually concluded with another posting which did not come as unwelcome as it included promotion to air commodore. It was to be the exercise controller in the United Kingdom Commanders in Chief Committee at Headquarters UK Land Forces at Wilton. This posting was welcome since it involved a return to Wiltshire where my younger brother, David, was flying in the Army Air Corps. It was also within easy reach of Boscombe Down, of happy memory. The only downside was that on arrival in post I discovered that my first job would be to organise an exercise on Salisbury Plain for the Ace Mobile Force, AMF (Land) in about three weeks' time.

We were given a perfectly adequate married quarter on the Army patch at Bulbridge from where I could walk to work. Outside our house was an old fashioned electric street lamp post that our springer spaniel Robin used to decorate regularly by cocking his leg against it. One day in the process he gave a loud shriek and leapt into the air. On investigation the electricity company, who arrived very promptly, discovered that the metal door in the base of the post was live. This was quickly rectified but the dog never went near the post again!

The UKCICC posting was interesting in that I was given a lot of freedom over how I spent my time. Probably the most interesting part was organising UK-only exercises such as the signals exercise we organised with the Royal Navy in the Caribbean to test the long range communications equipment. I arranged to be accommodated in Tortola on Beef Island in the British Virgin Islands. The 'Treasure Isle Hotel' was very comfortable and had an excellent swimming pool which passed the time nicely. The Chief of Police in the BVI turned out to be a Welshman, so we got on well together, and there was sufficient time left to explore around some of the other islands in the BVI group. There was also time for a bit of sub-aqua training. This was good fun but I never really got to grips with the breathing regime. There was a short airstrip on Beef Island which was adequate for use by the Hercules in which we were travelling.

Another exercise took me to Antigua. English Harbour was fascinating and it was surprising to find so many ex RAF officers living on the island. I quickly got befriended and was very well looked after during my relatively short stay. One of the ex RAF types, a retired group captain, later came to stay with us with his wife in our married quarter at Bulbridge in Wilton. They were very pleased to see something of the UK again and to note any changes there had been since they had left a few years earlier. It was fortunately summer time so the smell their chain smoking left in the house was dispersed relatively quickly!

All too soon, in some ways, a posting notice arrived to take over as AOC (air officer commanding) in Cyprus. This sounded like good news, and so it turned out. The only down side was the lack of indigenous fixed wing aircraft under command. The only aircraft based at Akrotiri, the sole airfield in the command, were a squadron of Whirlwind helicopters. On this basis I was able to arrange a short helicopter familiarisation course at Ternhill before I took over. As a result I was able to solo in a Whirlwind shortly after arriving in Cyprus.

16

Cyprus

The AOC at the time lived in a nice house close to the beach, called Flagstaff House. This was a relic of the days when the Commander British Forces Cyprus was tied RAF and the One Star Army Commander Land Forces lived in Flagstaff House. When the commander became a rotating appointment he lived in Air House, as that was the larger and more prestigious of the two houses. This caused some confusion in that officers responding to an invitation from the general would automatically turn up at Flagstaff House, likewise those responding to an invitation from the AOC would turn up at Air House. This led to some embarrassment until the general and I agreed that we would hold our functions on the same evening and accept whoever turned up at the door. This worked very well and eventually the word got around and people learnt that the Army was living at Air House and the RAF at Flagstaff House.

Another responsibility of the AOC was to be Deputy Commander of British Forces in Cyprus. This was an interesting feature of life and I was able to ensure that there would be no evidence of a possible khaki/light blue competition. There was enough productive work to avoid any petty rivalries that might tend to erupt, and I think it fair to say that the two services got on better together in Cyprus than they do today in many other places. I claim no great credit for this, a lot of it was to do with the wise governance of the General Commanding British Forces Cyprus, General Reynell Taylor late 4th/7th Dragoon Guards.

As an AOC I was entitled to a small personal staff. This consisted of a flight lieutenant admin ADC, sergeant admin, a corporal house steward, corporal cook and a corporal driver plus four local Cypriots who worked in the house and garden. I took over the current ADC when I arrived because he had not finished his tour in Cyprus so it was agreed that he would stay on with me on a provisional basis for as long as it took. It did not in fact take all that long because we never really saw eye to eye and after a while I requested a replacement. The solution was to find someone already on the island. There turned out to be a squadron leader admin, David Duckworth, in the headquarters who was coming up to being tour expired and who did not want to go home. He was posted in as my ADC and in fact it worked out beautifully. He was highly efficient and with a good sense of humour so we got on very well together and in fact I am still in touch with him via Christmas cards etc.

The corporal driver was responsible for the two staff cars, large Rovers with number plates RAF1 and RAF2. These were number plates issued by the Sovereign Bases Administration so at the time I must have been the only AOC in the world who had cars RAF1 and RAF2. It would not of course be possible in the UK, or in many other countries. Another perk of being AOC Cyprus was being issued with a Walther PP.32 semi-automatic pistol. This was a lovely little weapon and the ADC and I occasionally drew some ammunition from the armoury and had some competitive practice on the range. I was very sorry to hand it back when I left.

One pleasing feature of life on the island was the annual attachment of the Red Arrows, involving their final work up for display clearance for the coming season. They would spend a couple of weeks at Akrotiri practising every day and they added much to life on the island by their presence. They were incidentally very good publicity for the RAF on the island, so we welcomed their presence. In those days the team was flying the Folland Gnat aircraft which to my mind were in terms of appearance better suited to the displays than the Hawk.

Customarily the AOC gave a supper party for the Red Arrows during their stay and sometime after their visit Jackie was in the lavatory and on pulling some toilet paper off discovered written on about the third sheet down the following message!

Other squadrons also came to stay in Cyprus mainly for armament practice camps and I was lucky enough to scrounge a number of flights with the various Lighting and Phantom squadrons including one with Squadron Leader Steve Nicholl in a Phantom of 29 Squadron, Steve had been a student at Oxford UAS in my time there.

All went well and we were lucky in that we did not have any serious accidents, mainly because we had no fixed wing aircraft in the command. A Canberra on detachment from the UK crashed on take-off

The note found by Jackie in the lavatory.

in a sadly fatal accident but could not be held to be the responsibility of AOC Cyprus.

Another pleasing feature of Cyprus was the beach scene. It was one of the few places in the world where one could snow ski and water ski within hours of each other on the same day. The Troodos mountains in Cyprus went up to about 11,500 feet and with the correct winter conditions one could get sufficient snowfall for skiing to be possible and if the snow did arrive the services were prepared to set up a ski centre for uniformed personnel. This was very much appreciated by all and we were lucky to get enough snow in our spring in Cyprus to be able to ski for a couple of days. Water skiing was more readily available and if the conditions were right the sea could be calm enough first thing in the morning to allow skiing to take place. There were water ski clubs but the queues to get a tow were considerable and eventually I decided that the answer was to get my own speed boat. This I did and bought a 15 ft Taylor speed boat fitted with an Evinrude motor. This was kept in the water at Akrotiri, the only snag eventually turning out to be that the 55 horse power Evinrude motor was not powerful enough to pull me out of the water on one ski. It nevertheless provided a great deal of fun for all the family and was invaluable, especially when we had visitors. We would customarily take visitors water skiing first thing in the morning and then bring them back to Flagstaff House for a water ski breakfast which consisted of Buck's Fizz, bacon and eggs, and toast and marmalade. This was very much appreciated and helped to make up for the discomfort if any of the visitors had suffered a water ski enema. Details I will leave to your imagination.

A notable feature of life on the island whilst we were there was the fact that it was divided in two. As a result of the Turkish 'invasion' in 1974 there was a so called Green Line across the island with Turkish Cypriots to the north of it and Greek Cypriots to the south. There was still a lot of bad feeling between the two sides and the United Nations had a fairly sizeable contingent on the island which policed the Green Line. The general commanding the United Nations force was a very charming Irishman General Jim Quinn, so as I had been to Trinity College Dublin, we got on well together and his charming wife Mary was good enough to make me a present of some very handsome prints of my alma mater Trinity College Dublin which I still treasure. I was fortunate, because of my position as Deputy Commander British Forces, I was able to cross the Green Line and get into the Turkish zone when I wished. We did occasionally do this to go and stay the night in a borrowed flat in Kyrenia which was rather sad as the village was on the coast and all set up for mass tourism, the only problem being that at that time there weren't the tourists. Nevertheless the restaurants were all set up with tables facing the sea and one could enjoy very good meals in solitary peace and comfort.

Dinner parties were a frequent feature of our life at Flagstaff and Concorde regularly flew over with a sonic boom at about 8 p.m. local time on its way east. We always stood up and saluted it!

The climate in Cyprus attracted a regular stream of visitors, especially in the summer months, and many were welcomed to stay at Flagstaff House. They brought an interesting infusion of news from home and new topics for discussion.

A regular feature was concerts held at Curium the ancient Greco/Roman amphitheatre near Limassol. The RAF Central band paid an annual visit to Cyprus and the concert they put on at Curium was always a highlight of the year.

Another notable occasion was when the astronomer Patrick Moore came to visit and presented a concert of his favourite recorded music interspersed with comments on the night sky and identification of various space craft moving across the sky. For his return home we managed to arrange a helicopter flight to take him from Flagstaff House to Akrotiri. This was his first ever flight in a helicopter and he exposed a whole reel of film during the flight!

Her Royal Highness the Princess Anne visited the island during our time there, mainly in connection with the Royal Signals of which she is colonel-in-chief. To even things out between the services she spent the day at RAF Akrotiri and I had the honour of sitting next to her at lunch in the officers' mess.

Another regular visitor to the island was my commander in chief Air Chief Marshal Sir David Evans and his charming wife who were perfect guests and we were always sorry to see them leave.

A great pleasure for us was the opportunity for regular contact with the bishop of Cyprus and the Gulf, Len Ashton. Len had been the chaplain at Cranwell when I was a flying instructor there and eventually chaplain-in-chief to the RAF. Len was one of the most charming and entertaining people imaginable and was always a most welcome guest at Flagstaff House. He also gave some of the best sermons I have ever heard!

In October 1979 HMS *Bulwark* and RFA *Resource* visited Cyprus as part of a joint operation and Jackie and I were flown out by RN Helicopter to lunch on *Resource* where we enjoyed an excellent Chinese meal prepared by the Chinese crew.

The Navy also visited in June 1980 with two ships led by HMS *Galatea* commanded by Captain Robin Hogg. The ships' companies were entertained ashore by the Cypriots and so return hospitality was planned in the form of a reception on *Galatea*. Unfortunately on the day in question the sea was too rough to enable guests to be ferried out to *Galatea*. As a fall-back position we offered the Flagstaff House garden for the reception provided that catering etc. was done by the Royal Navy. This worked admirably and in due course Flagstaff was invaded by Royal Naval personnel setting up the party on the lawn. As part of the preparations a table was laid with nibbles including a large glass bowl full of crisps. This was left uncovered and unattended and just before the guests were due to arrive one of our house cats was spotted sitting in the middle of the crisps and helping himself! The damage was rapidly rectified and the party proceeded successfully. As a mark of gratitude Captain Hogg presented Jackie with an HMS *Galatea* bosuns' whistle.

During our time on Cyprus we were regularly entertained by Cypriot nationals including the owners of the two main wineries on the Island, ETKO and KEO. Our private motoring needs were also well looked after by Phivos Motors who did much business with the British Forces.

One of the wineries was kind enough to supply Jackie and me with a case of their new vintage, asking for our comments on the various varieties, it sometimes stretched the imagination to provide useful comments.

We also developed good relations with some of the Cypriot administrators particularly Yangos Antonio with whom I went fishing and fruit bat shooting. Fruit bats were considered as a pest by the Cypriot Government because they caused damage to the citrus fruit plantations which were a major export for Cyprus. The government therefore, from time to time, provided shotgun cartridges to be used for the purpose of thinning out the fruit bat population.

Fruit bats are nocturnal and during the day roost in colonies in caves, mostly sea caves. The form was that the guns embarked on a boat and positioned themselves opposite the entrance to the caves. A swimmer then went into the cave armed with a smoke flare. When the fruit bats appeared they were shot at, unfortunately no great damage was done to the population of bats because of inferior marksmanship! At least one visitor from the UK who happened to be staying at the time and so was included in the shooting party has regularly dined out on his account of shooting driven fruit bats!

Our three children were all at boarding schools in the UK during our time in Cyprus but they came out every holiday courtesy of the RAF 'school-run' from Brize Norton. They, of course, made the most of the swimming, water skiing, snow skiing, horse riding, tennis and all the other sports and pastimes available on the island.

During my tour in Cyprus I was honoured to be asked to be an ADC to Her Majesty the Queen, this appointment was for the duration of the tour and I was, obviously very happy to accept.

My time in Cyprus was coming to an end and I was eagerly awaiting a posting notice which eventually arrived. My next job was to be my final one in the Royal Air Force since I was due to retire in the autumn of 1984. The posting notice eventually arrived to go to RAF College Cranwell as deputy commandant. This suited me and the family beautifully as a last tour, with a few resident aircraft to fly to boot.

17

Cranwell

Our return to Cranwell for my last tour in the Royal Air Force was in many ways welcome. It was familiar territory and we were able to catch up with many old friends, perhaps in particular farmer friend Cis Bristow who lived on the edge of the airfield and was an old shooting companion.

Cranwell itself was a very different place from my time there as a flying instructor in the early 1960s. The RAF College had become an amalgam of various activities, a large base on which initial officer training formed only a part of the unit task. There were now four departments at the college each directed by a group captain.

The Department of Initial Officer Training ran the 18 week officer training course for a student population of mainly university cadet graduates, graduate direct entrants, non-graduate direct entrants and ex-service airmen. There were usually between 90 and 110 students on each course and a new intake arrived every six weeks. After graduation and commissioning from this course officers would go their separate ways for specialist training according to the branch they would join.

The headquarters university air squadrons, directly responsible to the commandant was also based in College Hall and was responsible for the organisation, control and administration of the 16 air squadrons located throughout the UK.

The Department of Air Warfare for which I was responsible, ran the five month air warfare course for group captains and wing commanders concerned with planning and execution of air operations and the 50 week General Duties Aerosystems course for less senior officers destined for jobs as systems specialists in operational requirements and research and development establishments. They were also responsible for several other shorter highly specialised courses to meet the increasingly complex needs of the RAF.

The Department of Specialist Ground Training provided the initial specialist training of engineer officers and supply officers. The training of secretarial officers for the administrative branch moved away from Cranwell to Hereford in 1980.

Cranwell also provides the airfield and facilities for a basic flying training school. Following their time at DIOT General Duties (GD) Pilots would attend the 36-week basic flying training course at one of the RAF's basic flying training schools (BFTSs), if not Cranwell then possibly Church Fenton or Linton-on-Ouse flying the Jet Provost. Cranwell also offered a shorter course of 30 weeks to those who already had substantial flying experience, for instance those who had been members of university air squadrons. Those pilots selected for fast jet training following their basic flying training could stay another 11 weeks at Cranwell before moving on to Valley to fly the Hawk.

There was also a support unit under the command of a wing commander which provided all the necessary administrative and support services to all the departments.

So Cranwell had grown out of all recognition while I had been away but the quality of training and the personnel were as high as ever.

We were allocated Bristol House, to live in on the edge of the North airfield and I had a small personal staff as well. The only snag was that I found myself saddled with bringing Cranwell up to scratch for its wartime role. It was due to operate a transport support unit and therefore became subject to NATO tactical evaluation (taceval) inspections. Until that time the war role had never been considered and we failed the first taceval which meant we had to be re-examined and a considerable amount of work had to go into get-ready for the re-examination. After much preparatory work and rehearsals we passed the next taceval satisfactorily. Subsequently a very senior officer, who had been a Cranwell cadet at one time, visited the college and objected to the war-like things that had appeared, such as barbed wire, in connection with our NATO role and the whole process was reversed.

I was fortunate in getting on very well with both commandants I served during my time at Cranwell. The first was Air Vice Marshal John Brownlow who was a fellow test pilot and had a keen interest in gliding, so we had much background in common. He also owned a villa on a small complex at Los Gigantes on the island of Tenerife which he kindly loaned us for a holiday which we much enjoyed.

The second commandant was Air Vice Marshal Richard Peirse. Dickie, as he was known, came from a distinguished Air Force family and co-incidentally had served a spell as station commander at RAF Waddington a short distance from Cranwell. Dickie was a very urbane and relaxed individual with a delightful sense of humour and like John Brownlow left me very much alone to get on with my job.

The Cranwell shoot was still going strong and I happily re-joined and was fortunate enough to receive a number of invitations locally, some of which were for the commandant who did not shoot, and who kindly therefore passed on the invitations to me. It was not long before Cis Bristow took ill and sadly, died in hospital. I agreed with his widow to buy Cis's Purdey shotgun, it was already fairly ancient having been built in 1900 but was in pretty good order apart from the barrels being pitted as a result of rust. It also had a very short stock which was cracked so I decided I would have it re-stocked left handed, because I had recently changed hands. Rather than take it to Purdeys who would have charged a fortune for the work I located a gunsmith locally, in fact in Ancaster, called Geoff Mobbs, who traded as Ancaster Guns. Geoff was a remarkable character, he was a self-taught gunsmith having started doing small repairs for his own guns and for his friends. This led to an increasing interest in the business and he set himself up as an independent gunsmith. He was entirely self-trained and his day-job was as a dispenser in Boots the Chemist. He was nevertheless a brilliant craftsman and did a wonderful job in renovating the Purdey, which emerged looking brand new. I used it happily for some time and only finally sold it when little bits of the action were starting to break—presumably suffering from 100 year metal fatigue.

By the time I retired from the RAF and moved to Wiltshire I needed to find another gunsmith to look after the Purdey and located a man called Mark Crudginton who came of the well-known firm of gunmakers in Bath. Mark had set himself up in a workshop near Wootton Rivers in Wiltshire and happily took on the care of the Purdey. I eventually sold the Purdey, sadly, in 2013 having enjoyed many happy seasons with it. I finally retired from game shooting in 2014 having been a happy member of the Field Barn Shoot near Dinton for 17 years.

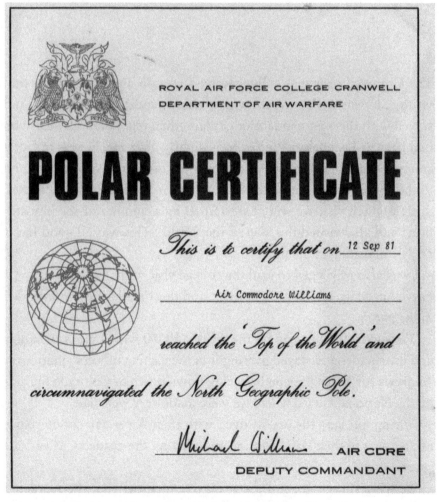

ROYAL AIR FORCE COLLEGE CRANWELL
DEPARTMENT OF AIR WARFARE

POLAR CERTIFICATE

This is to certify that on 12 Sep 81

Air Commodore Williams

reached the 'Top of the World' and circumnavigated the North Geographic Pole.

AIR CDRE
DEPUTY COMMANDANT

Polar certificate from College of Air Warfare visit to Norway.

18

Cranwell visits and Visitors

The Cranwell tour was enlivened by a certain amount of visits and visitors. I went to Dartmouth with a visiting cadets sporting team and stayed with the commandant or captain, then one Julian Oswald who had been at Beaudesert Prep School slightly after me, he was in fact a contemporary of my brother. Additionally I used to travel each autumn to the United States with a team from the Air Warfare College courses, during which visit we were entertained by a number of the industry firms and also visited the 'Top of the World'. This was all good fun if fairly exhausting at the time.

I was also privileged to lead the college visit to the United States Air Force Academy at Colorado Springs, and this time Jackie was included in the party.

We flew to Washington on the weekly VC10 with a party of cadets and instructors and stayed overnight in the visiting officers' quarters at Andrews Air Force Base before being flown down to Colorado Springs by the National Guard where we were made very welcome.

During our stay the cadets lived with their American counterparts taking part in their daily routine and playing the academy at various sports.

We were shown around the extensive facilities that the Academy enjoyed and taken into the Cheyenne Mountain complex, at that time the North American Defence (NORAD) command centre. We were wined and dined very well and all in all it was a most memorable and pleasurable visit. We had two days in Washington before returning to UK and that gave us time to visit the Air and Space Museum and catch up with some RAF friends, Geoff and Jane Glover who were serving in our embassy at the time.

Being the Royal Air Force College, Cranwell naturally enjoyed a fair number of visitors. It was customary to invite a VIP to review each passing out parade. Her Majesty the Queen visited us fairly regularly, often to take a passing out parade, usually accompanied by the Duke of Edinburgh. On those occasions the commandant accompanied the Queen for the day while I looked after the Duke of Edinburgh. Prince Philip did not always display any great enthusiasm for the occasion and I found it hard to sustain a relevant conversation over the course of the day. Nevertheless these days were a great privilege especially the inaugural 'Queen's Review' on 24 July 1981 which her Majesty had approved as the new title for the annual prize-giving parade previously called the College Review. This meant that Cranwell now had the equivalent of Dartmouth's Lord High Admiral's Parade and Sandhurst's Sovereigns Parade. It was a very special day.

One memorable passing out parade was taken by the then Prime Minister Margaret Thatcher. It was also customary to invite the VIP to plant a tree as part of the day's visit. The form was that a hole had been dug in the ground in the appropriate place and a sapling with roots had been placed in the hole and a heap of soil was piled onto plastic sheeting next to the hole. The VIP was then handed a highly polished shovel and invited to put some earth into the hole around the roots of the tree. The Prime Minister took the shovel and started to move earth into the hole and instead of the normal couple of shovel-fulls that was expected she continued, determined to get every single last scrap of earth into the hole. This she succeeded in doing then patted the earth down so that it was nice and smooth on the surface and handed back the shovel saying 'Right, that's that, what's next?' What was next was a visit to the York House Officer's Mess for coffee. The commandant put her into the car and climbed in beside her. When they got to the mess the car drew up and it was apparent that the Prime Minister was on the wrong side of the car, as a result of the driver going the wrong way around the roundabout outside the main entrance so that when the door was opened she got out and had to walk around the car to get into the mess. The commandant apologised to her and said 'I'm sorry Prime Minister I must have put you into the wrong side of the car'. She said to him, 'That's alright Commandant, everyone is entitled to one mistake a day.' As the commandant said later; 'There I was half an hour into the visit and I had already made my one mistake for the day.'

A regular summer occasion was the Old Cranwellian (OCA) weekend when previous students arrived to compete against the present college at various sports, cricket, tennis, clay pigeon shooting etc. These were always happy and relaxed occasions.

A 'one-off' visit was that of the Brough Superior Owners Club who brought some vintage machines and re-created Lawrence's famous race with an aircraft along the Cranwell to Lincoln road. The original race was recounted in his book *The Mint* and the original aircraft was a Bristol Fighter from RAF Digby. The Cranwell Flying Club Tiger Moth flown by myself and Group Captain Richard Joyce stood in on this occasion and as racing on the public roads was not on we just flew alongside the bikes. Some of the machines owners were fairly aged and quite frail and at least one of them was not sufficiently heavy to turn his engine over with the kick start, so a friend helped out and they all set off in convoy. The rig of the day seemed to be grey flannel trousers and cycle clips. The pictures were taken on the airfield.

Another notable visitor was astronaut Colonel James Irwin (Jim) who had been in the lunar module as part of the Apollo 15 mission to the moon in 1971. We entertained him to supper at Bristol House before he gave a very interesting lecture in College Hall during which he quoted from the poem *High Flight* by John Gillespie Magee. (Appendix E). Magee was a young American pilot who was serving with the Canadian Air Force and who was killed aged 19 in a Spitfire training accident in 1941 whilst flying from RAF Digby and was buried in Scopwick Churchyard. I mentioned this to Jim and offered to take him to see the grave on which is engraved the first and last lines of the poem, this we did the following day; Jim was fascinated and took many photos. He had founded the High Flight Foundation in 1972 which took inspiration from the poem and continued to spread Christian values until his death in 1991. He and I had stayed in touch for some years.

Coming towards the end of my RAF career I wanted my final flight to be a solo and on 9 April 1983 I flew a Chipmunk for an uneventful 30 minutes around the airfield, having been cleared earlier that day by Group Captain Flying Richard Joyce.

19

Life after the RAF

When the time came to look forward to the end of my time at Cranwell which would also be the end of my Royal Air Force service, I was having to start thinking about what to do afterwards. I needed a fairly lucrative job as I would have a new mortgage and three children still in education. After many applications I was offered a job with terms that I really couldn't refuse, it was with a company called STC Components Limited, based in Harlow, Essex. I would have to live within 15 miles of Harlow so we started a search on the outside of the 15 mile ring. The job was as management development manager. The main *raison d'être* was that the managing director was concerned about the fact that his unit, i.e. factory managers, had a working life of only about six months before they retired or had to be moved. The job of the management development manager would be to improve this life expectancy. STC was a spin-off from ITT and retained ITT's ruthless culture, developed by one Harold Geneen. I felt quite early on that this culture contributed to the relatively short life expectancy of the unit managers.

The job included a fully expensed car, a good perk and we found a house at Rickling Green close to Saffron Walden which suited perfectly. I made the mistake, which I had warned many people against over the years, of commuting some of pension to help pay for the new house. I wish now that I had heeded my own advice. There is no way in retrospect that one can replace a commuted pension that is index-linked. The job proved interesting, if not entirely satisfying, and it was not too disappointing when the firm collapsed after a year or so, making all the staff redundant. After handing in my company car, I took up a job with Midland Bank in the City. It was as part of a tri-service team in the export finance department whose aim was to identify British defence firms that stood a reasonable chance of winning an export contract, so that Midland Bank could get alongside them and help with imaginative financing of the deal.

The team had recently come to the attention of certain parts of the press, partly because of its dealings with a company called Astra Holdings, some of whose business was regarded as 'black'.

During the course of my work in the City I came across an ex Royal Naval officer, one Commander John Hamilton, who, after leaving the Navy had qualified as a solicitor. He developed an interest in management and eventually established his own company John Hamilton Associates (JHA) to advise on management development in solicitors' practices; they also did a little recruiting for solicitors and their support staff. At that time many solicitors' practices were deciding that it was it not best use of partners' valuable fee-earning time for them to spend it managing the practice. There was therefore an interest in management structures which off-loaded partners from management without entirely removing them from decisions on management processes. John Hamilton was in an ideal position to advise on management structures and, if necessary, to populate the offices with the right people, many of them ex-service. At the time JHA rented a one-room office in the City and because the main office was in Guildford John was looking for someone to visit it every day and collect the mail etc. This I agreed to do for him on my way home from my work with Midland Bank. My role with JHA increased and when the Midland Bank job came to an end I joined them as a consultant and eventually managed the London Office—by that time several rooms.

20

Wiltshire

By the middle of 1988 we had grown a little tired of living in Essex and we seemed to be spending a lot of time and weekends on the newly-opened M25 going down to Wiltshire to see friends and relatives. By then my brother was living with his second wife in Stoford in the Wylye valley and both Jackie and I felt that it was time to move and we agreed on Wiltshire. My work was now done mainly at home and in London and so we needed to be within reasonable commuting distance from Salisbury or Grateley for trains to Waterloo.

Jackie put her considerable estate agent skills to work by taking trips to Wiltshire for a few days at a time looking for a suitable house.

Eventually she arrived home saying that she had found somewhere. I asked where it was, she said Wylye, and I remembered the Bell Inn and the chalk stream. We drove down to Wylye and down Church Street nearly as far as we could go. She pointed at a half built house and said that is it.

'We will have a say in how it is finished off' she explained, I thought it looked OK but was worried about a small field on the other side of the lane, 'what if that gets built on?' I asked. 'Well, we have the option to buy it' was the reply. I said 'hang on isn't that the river at the end of the field?' She said 'yes'. 'Does the fishing go with it?' I asked. 'Yes' she replied. I said 'OK, let's do it'. In retrospect, one of the best decisions

Above left: Mother, Father, brother David and Self; Haverfordwest 1935.

Above right: The family home, Cranleigh, Haverfordwest 1940.

Below left: 2nd Lt Michael Williams Royal Artillery 1948.

Below right: Marlborough College Shooting Team 1945.

Trinity College Dublin 1951.

Above: No. 15 Hunter Course Chivenor 1956: Back Row: P/O McLoughlin, P/O Waterstone, F/O Stark, F/O Topping, F/O Williams, F/O Bell, P/O Marshall, P/O Brown. Front Row: P/O Biddescombe, P/O McEvoy, P/O Hann, Flt/Lt Henderson, Flt/Lt Murray, P/O Whittingham, P/O Wright, P/O Hawtin.

Left: Escape and evasion exercise Al Shepherd and self Hullavington 1954.

2 Litre low chassis Lagonda Chivenor 1956.

Above and below: 245 Squadron Meteors Stradishall, summer of 1957. (*IWM*)

Hunter off end of runway in field, Stradishall 1957.

Above: Hunter off end of runway in field, through gap in hedge Stradishall 1957.

Below: Waterbeach 1958.

Above: Hunter Simulator Course Chivenor 1957: Smith 43 Sqn, Vaughan 56 Sqn, Williams 63 Sqn, Clayton Jones 111 Sqn, Aldridge 111Sqn, Edwards 92 Sqn. (*IWM*)

Below: 63 Squadron Hunter at London Airport (now Heathrow) for Battle of Britain display 19-22 September 1958; the Blackburn Beverley in the background.

Above left: Wedding at Ruskington May 1965.

Above right: Flight Lieutenant Williams Cranwell 1960. (*Cartoon by Pat Rooney*)

Below: Till Cottage, our first home.

Maala Aden 1966.

Above left: Tarshyne Beach, Aden 1966.

Above right: The Aden Flood 1967.

The Aden Flood 1967.

Above: The Outspan Hotel, Kenya 1967.

Below: Ghillies outside the Isaak Walton Hotel, Embu, Kenya 1967.

The Isaak Walton Hotel, Embu, Kenya 1967.

Above: Oxford University Air Squadron Headquarters, Old Hangar, Manor Road, Oxford 1968.

Below: Presentation of Cooper Aerobatic Trophy to OUAS, Cadets Bernie Fitchct and Steve Nichol and self. 1968.

Above left: OUAS Chipmunks flying to Henlow, self in lead plane, 1968.

Above right: Her Majesty Queen Elizabeth the Queen Mother with self at Little Rissington 1974.(*IWM and Buckingham Palace*)

CFS visit to the Royal Australian Air Force base East Sale, Macchi 326 in the background. 1976. (*RAAF*)

RAF Little Rissington exercise their freedom of Cheltenham. Parade through the streets June 1974; Air Commodore John Severne, Mayor of Cheltenham and self taking the salute.

Above: The Spitfire Gate Guardian outside the station commander's office Little Rissington.

Below: Flight Lieutenant Frederick the Pelican on parade, Little Rissington.

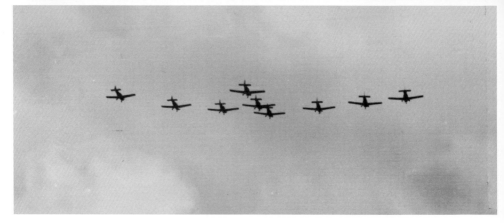

The final farewell to Rissy, formation of Jet Provosts away to Cranwell 1976.

Above: Station staff watching the last flight, Little Rissington 1976.

Left: Official Portrait of AOC Cyprus. 1979.

Flagstaff House Episkopi, AOC's official residence.

Above: Flagstaff House Family and staff.

Below: Patrick Moore and self with Whirlwind Helicopter at Flagstaff. (*IWM*)

Above left: Self and wife in the garden Flagstaff.

Above right and below: Recreation of the race between T. E. Lawrence (Aircraftsman Ross) and a motorcycle from Cranwell to Lincoln from his book The Mint. Brough Superior motorbike and Tiger Moth flown by Group Captain Richard Joyce and self. 1983.

Above: USAFA Colorado Springs, official visit March 1983, Jackie and Self with Commandant of Academy.

Below: Dining in night at USAFA Colorado Springs, official visit March 1983.

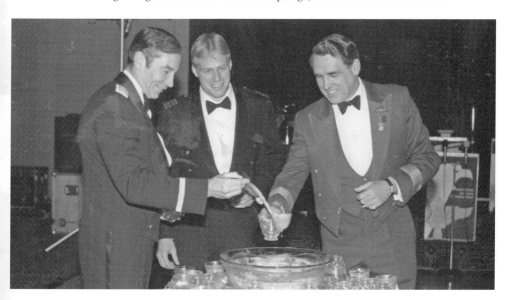

Below: Bristol House Cranwell, deputy commandant's residence.

Self fishing for salmon in the Eachaig, 2007.

Above: Gundogs in the garden at Wylye, Barney, Teal and Sage, 2010.

Below: Family and friends celebrate our golden wedding Wylye, May 2015.

we have ever made. In particular after my stroke in 2012 it was easily converted to being wheelchair-friendly whereas some of the picturesque cottages we might have bought would have been impossible

So it was that we came to move in 1989; the house in Rickling Green sold quickly to a neighbour which was a relief as it saved having to pay agents' fees.

When we moved I was still doing three days a week in London looking after John Hamilton's London office. I had also developed a few more consultancy occupations one of them being with an executive search (head-hunters) in London called EAL International. It was run by a baronet, Sir Geoffrey Errington, and one of the directors was a man named Slim, a son of the famous Second World War general. I only worked part time for EAL but it did lead to other contacts and I started to do some work in journalism by becoming the air editor of *Defence Systems International* a journal published by the Sterling Group in London. This involved deciding on the air content and then commissioning the necessary articles. It was interesting work, much of which could be done from home.

I also took up a part-time consultancy with a firm called Hoybond. Hoybond was in the camouflage or signature-management business. At one stage it involved a visit to South Korea to advise their air force on signature reduction for their airfields. Hoybond was eventually taken over by Dowty and I went with them to consult for what became Dowty Hoybond.

Eventually I joined forces with an ex-army officer Brigadier Gerald Blakey retired, as the air editor for the quarterly journal *Defence Procurement Analysis*. This involved keeping up with the latest developments in the market and going to air shows at Paris and Farnborough. All the publications mentioned were financed by advertising by a team of salesmen in the publisher's office who spent most of their time on the telephone to potential advertisers. The publishing line eventually came to an end when the internet became widespread and much of the information we were collating could be found online. In fact I would have welcomed a rather earlier introduction of email because much of the editorial matter that I assembled was coming in to me by fax which was unwieldy and required retyping.

The house in Wylye proved a great success and I soon assembled a portfolio of fishing extra to my 100 yards plus eventually membership of a small game shoot near Dinton.

By early 1997 John Hamilton had decided to close his London office so my need to be in the capital three times a week disappeared. I began to think about using my enthusiasm for fly fishing positively and looked around for opportunities. I decided to try to turn my lifelong interest to profitable use and contacted a firm called Orvis who were then based in Nether Wallop Mill near Stockbridge. It so happened that the head ghillie of Orvis was one Jim Haddrell whom I had met many years previously in a pigeon shooting context. I contacted Jim and eventually was signed up as an Orvis ghillie on the chalk streams in Hampshire and Wiltshire. A ghillie is a Scottish term for a guide.

The work consisted of looking after Orvis clients who had signed up for a day's trout fly fishing, helping them to catch fish and generally assisting. Starting as self-employed eventually Orvis were required by HMRC to put me on the staff which was not a disadvantage in that it gave me a sizeable discount on the purchase of Orvis goods. The Orvis work lasted until the end of the 2012 season when I retired having found that the work was not as pleasant as it once had been.

I met many interesting people with Orvis and fished in many very pleasant places. All in all I did 292 ghillie days for Orvis; a mixture of guiding and tuition, involving, perhaps 500 different people. I also attended a number of Open Days, shows, etc. on behalf of the firm. I learned a lot and found out the truth of the old saying that the best way to learn a skill is to try to teach it.

I was fortunate to avoid any health problems with elderly clients such as strokes or heart attacks, although I did attend a course learning how to recognise the symptoms and what action to take.

Apart from voluntarily retiring at the end of the 2012 season, I would have been prevented from carrying on guiding for Orvis by my own stroke in November 2012, after which I was confined to a wheelchair.

Orvis is an interesting company founded in the United States in 1856 and claiming to be the oldest fishing tackle manufacturer still in business. They moved into the UK in 1982 and took over an existing mail order tackle business called Dermot Wilson which he had built up with his wife Renie. He was the forerunner of all the main mail order businesses today. He had a quirky catalogue which was fun and he operated from Nether Wallop. Jim Haddrell was inherited from Dermot Wilson when Orvis came in, in 1982. Haddrell and Wilson were both Army Green Jackets.

When Orvis bought out the business they also bought a half-mile stretch of the Test river (a beat) at Kimbridge, and a beat on the Itchen at Abbots Worthy. Kimbridge was closer than Abbots Worthy. The Orvis beat at Kimbridge was known as the 'ginger beer beat' because at the top of it water came over a weir and formed foam which in the early days made it look like the only fizzy drink that was on the market i.e. ginger beer.

Orvis also took over two beats on the Test at Timsbury. When I started with Orvis the Test beats generally had good fly-life but by 2012 the fly life had diminished making fly fishing more difficult.

I was sorry to have to leave Orvis which was a very good company to work for, and with whom I spent many happy days on the river bank. Clients were mainly British, with a few Americans. I also eventually got involved in teaching on one-to-one tuition days on the Test or the Itchen. These were interesting and challenging because one wanted the pupil however inexperienced, to catch fish.

Some clients were kind enough to write to Orvis thanking them for the day and occasionally making mention of the ghillie, one letter saying 'the ghillie Michael was inspirational' which Orvis could then use on their publicity.

A typical day would start by meeting the customer at the shop in Stockbridge or on the beat. Customers could bring their own tackle and I would have the latest rods for them to try out, and may be encouraged to buy. Each beat would have hotspots to try for fish. At peak season I was ghillying two or three days a week, so I got a good idea of the river.

Sometimes they brought their own lunch, sometimes they went to a pub sometimes inviting me to join them, but I preferred not to eat my tip!

Jim Haddrell had been in the Far East and he had a hard war. One day at Kimbridge he had as a sole guest a retired general and he briefed the general in advance of all the hotspots and where to go, the general said 'you are in command today Jim, lead from the front,' Jim replied 'in all my years in the Army, General, I never saw anyone in command anywhere near the front.' This was greeted with hilarity and they enjoyed a good day together.

The decline in the fly life evident in my later years was caused by perhaps water quality, or due to regular stocking with hungry fish which gobbled up all the larvae!

After living in Wylye for a while I started to go beating on a game shoot at Ballington Manor a couple of miles downstream from Wylye. In due course Ballington Manor and the shoot were sold to a man called John Tremlett. John turned out to be the brother of Edward Tremlett with whom I had shared a study in Littlefield House when we were both at Marlborough College. I had in fact stayed for a few days with the Tremlett family when they lived in Exmouth.

John Tremlett and his wife Pauline became good friends and John invited me to organise and manage the fishing on the river Wylye at Ballington, this I happily did for some years. I set up a small syndicate of eight rods several of whom were employed at the Moorfields Eye Hospital in London and who enjoyed coming down at weekends, sometimes bringing their families for a break from the pressures of London. We stocked the river with takeable brown trout and regularly electro-fished to remove the pike. I relinquished the management roll after a few years finding that it occupied too much of my time with weed cutting etc. during the busy summer months. The stocking arrangements continued until a family of otters arrived on the river and found easy pickings amongst the naïve stock fish, so stocking was discontinued. The river is now being allowed to return to its natural unstocked state and it seems likely that the syndicate will no longer be viable.

I was already engaged in beating on shoot days at Ballington before the arrival of the Tremletts and Jackie was picking up with our three Labradors and this continued very enjoyably under the new management.

As a result of my interest in game shooting becoming known I was invited to be a founder member of a new shooting syndicate being formed to shoot over land at Field Barn, Dinton just over the hill from Wylye. This proved very successful and as it was run on a self-help basis I got involved in the game keeping including looking after the 700 pheasants and 200 partridge we put out each year.

The Field Barn Shoot was a friendly shoot; popular with guests because it was seen to be a traditional 'family style' shoot as opposed to the many large commercial shoots in the area, this was in no small part due to the Fry family who farmed the land on which we shot and to Mike Vesey who ran the syndicate.

All guns, beaters and pickers-up happily ate their picnic lunches together in a disused milking parlour and after the last drive returned for tea and cake and a chat about the success or otherwise of the day. I was sad to have to retire when I became wheelchair bound.

In about 1990 I came across an advert in the *Shooting Times* for a shoot manager in Wiltshire and thought it might be interesting so I applied. The contact was one Bruce Gauntlett who farmed at Wootton Rivers near Marlborough and who had started a company with David Rogers called the Alternative Shooting Company (ASC). They were the initiators of simulated game shooting using clay pigeons. The concept was original and the success of the company's events was mainly down to the very powerful clay traps that Bruce designed and had built. The events could be run on different estates at all times of the year and days were designed to simulate a real game shoot day as closely as possible with different drives and a good lunch if required. The concept proved popular and has been widely copied, but in my experience the copies are not satisfactory because they lacked the powerful traps used by the ASC.

Many syndicate shoots found the simulated days a good way to warm up for the shooting season and they were also popular with stag and hen parties.

The Alternative Shooting Company eventually ran down because of difference of opinion between Bruce and David Rogers about the way ahead. I had spent many happy days helping with ASC events at various different estates and stayed on with Bruce when he continued to run regular days single-handed.

As well as simulated shooting Bruce, for a time, ran major partridge shoot days with which both Jackie and I helped in various ways. It was a busy, interesting and enjoyable time.

We now had three working Labradors and were picking up on various local shoots as well as for Bruce, three or four days a week. Picking up duties gradually decreased due to changes on shoots, gamekeepers etc.

21

Travels

It was during this time that Jackie and I decided that as we were both now more or less retired and with our children settled we should do some travelling. We visited Paris, one of our favourite cities several times, sometimes combining it with the Paris Air Show if I was involved with representing an aircraft firm there and eventually to visit our daughter Jane who worked there for a while. The Eurostar was at that time based in Waterloo and the Salisbury trains went into Waterloo so it was very convenient to be able to walk from one train to another and on occasion to have breakfast in Wylye and lunch in Paris or vice-versa!

We were also lucky enough to have the use of a house in the Gers department of the Midi-Pyrenees which was owned by John Hamilton who has been mentioned previously. We would take the car across on the ferry and wander down through France to stay a week or so in this lovely and very unspoilt part of the country.

Ireland was another favourite particularly the Ring of Kerry area and we did several trips to Waterville staying at the Lakelands Farm Hotel on the banks of Lough Currane and making use of the fishing and guides from there.

We also went to Pembrokeshire every year staying in our Holiday Property Bond accommodation at St Brides Castle which provided a good base with all the on-site facilities, swimming pool, restaurant etc. but left us free to do our thing and visit old friends and old haunts.

Scotland was always on the list and every year we went up to Argyle where I had bought a fishing time share on the River Eachaig a three-mile-long spate river which flows from Loch Eck to the head of Holy Loch and thence to the Firth of Clyde. It had a good run of salmon and I was lucky enough to catch one occasionally.

Although we had both visited the United States we had never spent time in Florida and the Everglades had always been on Jackie's 'wish list', so in 2002 we booked a house on the outskirts of Kissimmee which was in a small complex on the edge of a lake. Each house had its own small swimming pool, all very tightly fenced against an alligator dropping in. We enjoyed our stay, but found that so much of Florida was a building site at that time that we wondered when it would stop! The Everglades were the only place that we found any awareness of the problems that came with overdevelopment, and the greatest concern was lack of water, the Everglades is drying out! Just before we arrived in Kissimmee there had been a tornado and when visited the local airfield to see the collection of vintage aircraft we noted that one of the hangars was flattened to a height of about 10 feet and we were told that there were still four aircraft in it!

We visited Dubai to see daughter Jane who was working there and living in a nice flat in a block with its own pool which we made good use of. This was a time when the Gulf States generally and Dubai in particular were just emerging as a tourist destination. It was before the really major developments such at the Burj Khalifa and the Palm Jebel Ali had been thought of, but even so the existing hotels, beach clubs and shopping malls were something to behold! We hired a car and did a trip up country to stay at the Hatta Fort Hotel for a few days, whilst there we hired a 4 × 4 with driver for a trip into the mountains including a swim in the fresh water pools. We also explored Sharjah and Abu Dhabi, including the camel market which was very noisy and smelly!

We enjoyed a lovely week in Orkney with our son Peter and his family and learnt much about the ancient and recent history of this fascinating part of the UK. Scapa Flow and the sunken German fleet and Skara Brae with its ancient houses, the impressive standing stones at the Ring of Brodgar, the Churchill Barriers and the wonderful Italian Chapel were all amazing and only part of the wonder of the islands. There are also great crafts being practised today, the Hoxa Tapestry Gallery and the silversmiths making beautiful original pieces. The Orkney Agricultural Show was on the week we were there and it was a great day out with lots of animals, farm shops etc.

Other parts of the UK which we did not know and decided to explore were Anglesey. I had landed at RAF Valley a few times but never got off the airfield! Unfortunately the fog was down for most of our stay so we still did not see much of the island, but did drive around the Llyn peninsular and the foothills of the Snowdonia range. Sadly not one of our better trips!

Herefordshire and the mid-Wales borders gave us another happy break and we wandered around the areas lovely old towns and particularly enjoyed the visit and tour of Weston's Cider premises, especially the free tasting!

Our main trip was one that had long been thought about—New Zealand. We decided that we would make it into a round the world journey; and we planned to stay four weeks in New Zealand and would be away for six weeks altogether. This is the account written at the time:

22

New Zealand Saga 1999

19 February 1999—D-Day

Up betimes to get to Heathrow the required three hours before departure on Singapore Airlines SQ319 Boeing 747 to Singapore. 20 minutes late leaving LHR but caught that up on the way and had no problem making the connecting 767 to Hong Kong. The new HK airport, Chek Lap Kok, is fantastic, huge and futuristic and at present much underused, partly because it was designed to allow for considerable growth in traffic (up to 35 million passengers a year) and partly because the landing charges have been raised about 40 per cent above those for Kai Tak which has resulted in a number of airlines boycotting it. An enormous amount of new building is going on between the airport and Kowloon and we were fascinated to see that the scaffolding is all made of bamboo, even for the 'skyscrapers'. Apparently it is a government regulation that only bamboo is used.

The Hotel Metropole in downtown Kowloon was modern, comfortable and a good base for three nights. On our first day we went up to the Peak to meet and have lunch with our next door neighbours in Wylye, George and Daphne Hodgkinson! Their son David is based in Hong Kong, working for the HSBC, and George had been stationed there during his early Army service so we got a unique insight into the changes that have taken place in the Colony and since it became a Special Administrative Region of China in 1997. In fact Mike was so enthused that he bought Chris Patten's book *East and West* (in paperback—Mike is Welsh) and spent subsequent flights buried in it. We lunched in the restaurant at the top terminal of the Peak Tram with a wonderful view over Hong Kong and afterwards travelled down on the Tram to catch the Star Ferry across the harbour. A trip around the harbour on a Junk is a tourist 'must' so we paid our dues and saw the old airport and the floating villages of the fishing communities as well as the firing of the noon-day gun.

One evening we decided to have dinner in one of the hotel restaurants and on entering found that we were two of only about a dozen western faces in the crowded room, this we took as a good omen hoping that we would have a proper Chinese meal. To our surprise we found that the form was cook it yourself. We were presented with a small spirit stove and a bamboo steamer. We then had to help ourselves from a laden table which had some familiar and some strange ingredients. We were fortunate to share our table with a charming local couple who turned out to be students eager to try out their English and they showed us how to deal with cooking our meal. The result was surprisingly edible, due mainly to our two new friends!

Hong Kong in general proved a little disappointing, probably mainly because its economy is currently in recession. Certainly it did not have the air of bustling prosperity it is famed for, and shopkeepers were complaining about a lack of tourists. Also prices in the shops are not the bargain they used to be and the locals were saying that now the place to go for cheap goods is Macau, about 40 miles by sea from Hong Kong. Macau is being handed back to China by Portugal in December 1999, to become another SAR, so it is possible that things might change there as well.

Perhaps the overwhelming impression of Hong Kong is how fast it has grown, and continues to grow, and we were pleased to see it (for the first time) before its colonial character changes too much. A fascinating place, but not one in which either of us would care to live, or indeed have lived.

Flight NZ78, a 767-300, from Hong Kong to Auckland was comfortable and punctual. The Captain was an ex-RNZAF C-130 pilot and the co-pilot ex-Australian Navy helicopters. Flight time 10 hours 40, much over sea and on only two engines. ETOPS (Extended-range Twin-engine Operational Performance Standards) is a wonderful thing!

We had pre-booked a room at a motel near the airport in Auckland, which was adequate and picked up our Avis hire car, a Toyota Camry 3 litre V6 auto with air conditioning. Next day on the road, via Hamilton, to our friends Ian and Pat Thorpe who live on Lake Tarawera, near Rotorua. Ian was in the New Zealand Army and he and Mike did the Joint Services Staff College at Latimer together in 1969/70. They discovered a mutual interest in fishing and Mike took Ian for a day on the Windrush in April 1970, just before Ian had to return to New Zealand. It was bitterly cold, blowing a gale, and they struggled to catch anything—ending up with one miserable fish about 6 inches long. When he got back to New Zealand, Ian was kind enough to send Mike a mouth-watering book on trout fishing in New Zealand and was rash enough to invite us to stay in his cottage on Lake Tarawera if we ever came to New Zealand. Little did Ian realise that nearly 30 years later Mike would get in contact again and take him up on his offer!

Ian and Pat were the soul of kindness. Since 1969 they have built a house in the grounds of their original cottage, where they now live; it is idyllic. Ian had an interesting military career, being involved in every campaign to which New Zealand contributed forces from Korea onwards. His last tour, as a brigadier, was in Fiji and after retirement he was asked back there to set up and run a staff college—so what they don't know about the South Pacific is not worth knowing.

While fishing was obviously of interest, Mike had been gracious enough to concede that it would not be top priority on the trip, which was probably just as well because we arrived at the end of a very dry summer and the river fishing was not up to much in many places. On Lake Tarawera the thermocline was down at 75 feet, and therefore all the fish below that level, so the only way of catching anything was by trolling with steel lines and spinners. Not very exciting but Ian and

Mike succeeded in hauling up two rainbows on early morning sessions, biggest 4½ lbs.

The whole of the Tarawera area is of volcanic origin and the most recent eruption was in 1886, when 189 people were killed. This massive eruption buried a vast area around Mount Tarawera including the Pink and White terraces which had been a major tourist attraction in the area. One of the buried villages, Te Wairoa, has been excavated and is now open to tourists, the museum there gave a very clear picture of life in the village before the eruption and some harrowing accounts from the survivors. There is still a lot of volcanic activity in the area, especially round Rotorua, and Lake Tarawera has its own showpiece the Hot Beach, or as Mike christened it 'Kiriwhirangi' which is Maori for 'beach of the boiled foot'. The water on the shoreline in that area is too hot for comfort, but if you go through that to a depth of a foot or so it becomes quite cool. Apparently it bemuses dogs running along the beach when they come across it.

Apart from the delights of Lake Tarawera itself there is lots to see around that area. Rotorua's Agrodome has a daily show, mainly devoted to sheep, which is very slick and entertaining, with highly trained sheep which play their part perfectly, even with Huntaways standing on their backs. During the performance we attended there was a power cut (genuine it seemed) so we were able to see a demonstration of shearing with blades which is not normally included when there is electricity to power the shears. The museum, in what used to be the old Bath House, was informative on the subject of volcanoes and The Pig and Whistle, in the old police station, was a congenial lunch venue. The Whakarewa Thermal Reserve and Maori Cultural Centre were worth visiting for the hot geysers and mud holes, and especially for the Maori concert. It had not occurred to us that the traditional Maori 'Haka' was not only a threat display but also a method of exercising every muscle in the body, including the eyes and tongue, in preparation for battle.

During our time at Tarawera Mike had his only full day's fishing. We both went out with a guide named Dave Dawson to a river called the Whirinaki (all the Maori names took a bit of remembering!). We

were collected at 7 a.m. and driven out south of Rotorua for about
an hour in a Nissan Terrano 3 litre V6. The river was some way off
the beaten track and a little coloured by rain, although the day was
warm and sunny. Jackie decided not to fish so Mike set off with Dave
in borrowed 7mm neoprene waders (more boiled feet) to attack the
rainbows. It has to be said that the fishing, with weighted nymphs,
was not very exciting. After returning three small fish, Mike pricked a
biggish one which escaped and then it was time to go home, mindful of
the fact that we were paying pretty steeply by the hour. Dave D proved
an interesting companion. He runs a plumbing business employing
three men but in his time had been a helicopter 'jumper' (catching up
red deer stags for the deer farming market). He now flies Cessna 152s
and 172s and amongst other things owns a 750 Ducati.

The Thorpes have three children. Their son lives at Raglan and
is into the good life scene; he and his partner have two children. Of
the two daughters, the elder had ambitions of being an underwater
archaeologist but a diving accident put paid to that idea. The other
daughter, Jenny, now lives in Ian and Pat's cottage because her marriage
has broken up. She has two children, a boy, Levi, and a little girl, Aroha,
and a black lab called Tahi.

We could happily have spent more time than we did at Tarawera
but hospitality can be overstrained and there was lots more of New
Zealand still to see. So we left sadly and motored south lunching *en
route* at the Honey Hive bee centre and stopping to view the Huka
Falls, eventually arriving for an overnight stop at a B & B in Turangi
at the southern end of Lake Taupo, the Ika Lodge. The lodge was run
by a chap called Kerry Simpson who also does a lot of guiding; he
had just been out 17 days in a row when we got there. He said he
had guided for the Duchess of Kent at Huka Lodge and in Alaska,
and the day before his client had caught 32 fish between 1½ and 5
lbs. Valentino's restaurant in Turangi does very good Italian food.
Apparently a lot of Italians settled there to help dig the tunnels for the
hydro-electric systems, and some intermarried with the local Maoris,
the waitress was an Italian/Maori and a really beautiful girl (Jackie
wrote that bit!)

Next day we drove down to Napier, via a few of the vineyards/ wineries, and spent two nights B & B at a farm run by Tony and Sarah in Apley Road. Tony is a vet who emigrated from the UK. They are a pleasant couple who laid on a little supper party for us with some of their friends the night before we left. They have two cockerels who vied for the right to wake us up each morning, usually before dawn! We had supper in the local pub one night and ordered two beers—Tui (pronounced, we thought, tooee) this was greeted with a blank stare and on pointing to the appropriate pump were told 'Oh! You mean towee'. Anyway, we got our beer!

Napier had suffered a serious earthquake in 1930, and had to be extensively rebuilt, much of it in art deco style, which looks somewhat incongruous in a New Zealand setting. One of the things which had already struck us about New Zealand was the number of opossums which got run over on the roads. They are not indigenous but were introduced from Australia (the Australian bush tail opossum— Trichosurus Vulpecula) for the fur trade. They rapidly became a pest in the wild as they eat native trees and plants. 'Opossum World' just outside Napier gave a good impression of the unexpected consequences of their introduction and you could 'buy your opossum product and save a tree'. Napier also boasted a salt water aquarium where seawater is pumped around the tanks and a variety of species, including sharks, are kept.

We liked the Hawkes Bay area, particularly the wines. Many of the wineries do nice light lunches when you can also taste their wines, so we did quite a bit of that!

The night of Saturday was spent in Wellington at the Portland Hotel. Sadly it was pouring with rain which deterred us from seeing the sights of Wellington that day and on the Sunday we were off on the ferry at the crack of dawn—well almost. We handed in the Toyota Camry (with sadness) at Wellington and picked up a Holden at Picton which was adequate but not as nice as the Camry which, we discovered, was a two-category upgrade from what we had paid for. Sometimes you strike it lucky!

On Sunday we wandered down to Kaikoura and a nice motel, the Norfolk Pine, on the esplanade. We immediately liked Kaikoura, with its opportunities to go whale watching and swim with the dolphins etc., and made a mental note to go back there if time permitted. However we had agreed to go down to stay with William Gauntlett on Banks Peninsula so headed on down there next day.

Banks Peninsula is fabulous and Akaroa an ideal seaside holiday spot. While there we swam with the Hector's dolphins (very successful for both of us and only three people swimming which made it all a lot more personal). William Gauntlett is 86 and emigrated to Robinson's Bay from England, where he had farmed all his life, about 12 years ago. He is looked after by his married daughter Fiona who lives with her husband next door. Sadly, William's wife Eve died last year but he has got himself a rescue dog to keep him company and is coping very well. He still drives a car and could outpace us on the walks he took us on. A remarkable character.

After two very happy days on Banks Peninsula we motored down to Omarama where we had an introduction to Peter Casserly who runs the pub, the Omarama Inn. He has the distinction of holding to this day the world record for shearing with blades which he set about 20 years ago. He showed us around the high sheep stations at 'the Merino capital of the world' which struck us as just what we had imagined at least some of New Zealand would be like. They had had a bit of rain so were feeling a bit more cheerful but everything still looked fairly parched to us. On one of the evenings we were there the Otago Highlanders were playing in the Rugby Super 12 and as they are the local team and Peter has big screen TV in the bar it was quite a night, particularly as the Highlanders won!

Bruce Gauntlet, who had provided the introduction to Peter Casserly had asked us to have a look at the Ben Avon sheep station of Jim Morris. We spent a morning wandering up the lovely valley and called in to pay our respects to Jim—a huge man with a handshake like a vice. He turned out to be among other things a poet and signed two of his books, one for us and one for Bruce. Another sheep farmer at Omarama is Peter Patterson, whose station Peter Casserly drove us out to see in one of his two Land Rovers, both of which he was having to get rid of because they failed their MOT tests. At the side of Peter

Patterson's homestead is a hangar containing two helicopters and a light aircraft, the helicopters are used for gathering sheep from the tops, they load the sheep dogs into them and as they can't land on the rough ground on the tops, they hover and the dogs jump out and drive the sheep downhill—you can also shoot rabbits from them!

To our astonishment and considerable embarrassment, after staying in the pub for two days and booking drinks, meals, etc. to our room number, Peter steadfastly refused to accept any payment! So we have promised him a return match when he comes over to the World Shearing Championships (to be held at Edinburgh) in 2002 (as a spectator not a competitor—he says at the age of 50 he is over the top).

Next stop Oamaru, the Heritage Motel on Thames Highway for two nights. We liked Oamaru, it has some historic buildings in the dockside area—and some good pubs, especially Annie Flanagan's Irish pub which does a superb Irish stew and some very acceptable Guinness on draught. The motel is next door to the Meadowbank Bowling Club which lets residents use their bar. We popped in for a beer the first evening and got talking to some of the members which ended up in our having a session of bowling under instruction. Jackie turned out to be a natural and is talking about setting up a club in Wylye—the only problem is finding somewhere to play. More Super 12 on Sky Sports while we were here, NSW Warakahs v Chiefs and Hurricanes v Bulls. Not as exciting as the Highlanders, but a lot better than the Lennox Lewis/Evander Holyfield farce which was also on while we were there. The next afternoon went to Moeraki to see the 'unique' boulders on the beach which have been washed out of the cliffs by erosion. Curious but not all that thrilling. In the evening, after a second Irish Stew at Annie's we went to see if there were any yellow penguins coming up the beach. Two were visible on the beach and one on the cliffs a few feet from the path in the middle of moult. They have to come ashore for a couple of weeks to moult during which time they sit around in some discomfort not eating or able to do much. Later in the evening we watched the blue penguins emerging from the sea and making their way up the cliffs to their roosting places. There is a grandstand, floodlights and a commentary, none of which seem to bother the penguins of which we must have seen a dozen or more.

But Kaikoura was calling so we headed north round Christchurch (it was now Monday 15 March) towards Timaru where we thought we might spend the night. On the way a stop at Timuka revealed that close by, at Waitohi, was a memorial to one Richard Pearse who is reputed to have flown a powered aircraft in March 1903, i.e. some nine months before the Wright brothers. We had to go and look and very interesting it turned out to be because if the model on the memorial is accurate (about which there is doubt) then Pearse's aircraft had ailerons for lateral control rather than the wing warping used by Wilbur and Orville Wright. It seemed extraordinary that Pearse's achievement was not more widely known about, but when we asked about him at the RNZAF Museum at Wigram later there was considerable scepticism. Thence to Geraldine to the Vintage Car & Machinery museum. There seemed to be quite a lot of these in New Zealand, and also quite a lot of fairly ancient vehicles still in daily use. It was explained that corrosion is not so much of a problem in New Zealand because of generally low humidity and the fact that the roads are not treated with salt to prevent icing. Pressing on through Methven and the spectacular Rakaia Gorge we ended up spending the night at the Broadview Motel at Cheviot which was comfortable if undistinguished as was dinner at the Teviot Hotel (recommended by the motel) whose only real advantage was that it was in walking distance.

And so next day the short step to Kaikoura.

On the road into Kaikoura we passed the airport but decided not to, but to take a whale watching flight in a Nomad. The whole thing was very professional with 45 minutes airborne and an informed commentary by the pilot. We and about seven other passengers saw two sperm whales and a great gaggle (called a pod) of about 500 dusky dolphins. They are bigger than the Hector's dolphins we swam with at Akaroa and there are more of them. The flight was good value and gave an excellent impression of the size of the whales. The aircraft does not communicate directly with the two catamarans which also go out whale watching from Kaikoura, but they know that when the Nomad descends from its search altitude of 1,500 ft to its minimum height of 500 ft it has spotted a whale so they chase after it. While we were at the airport Mike spotted an offer of a half hour in a Cessna 152 for 'only' 69 dollars and his eyes were seen to light up—but he resisted the temptation (temporarily).

We had booked into the same motel in Kaikoura that we had stayed at before (the devil you know.....) which had the benefit that they had just called off their boycott of Sky TV and we were therefore able to keep up with Super 12 progress. That afternoon we booked up for a whale watching trip in a catamaran the next day and for a sea fishing trip the day after. Kaikoura must be one of the seafood capitals of the world—the crayfish are particularly delicious as is the seafood chowder. We tried not to eat out every single night of our trip but to have the occasional 'feast' in our motel, which is one advantage of motels over B & Bs. In fact although we had originally envisaged staying most nights in B & B we ended up more inclined to motels.

The weather was fairly warm in Kaikoura and Mike was even persuaded to buy (and wear) some shorts (almost unheard of says Jackie), on the other hand Jackie bought a fleece. The whale watching by boat was also very professionally organised and most successful. We saw four whales and watched them blowing and eventually diving. We had not realised that they dived vertically down, head first, and ascended the same way, or that they can dive to 3,000 ft and stay under for 20 minutes. Once again the whales do not seem to mind the attention of the boats and the operators do try to minimise any disturbance. After all, it is in their interests to do so. Everyone on each trip can buy for 10 dollars a photo of their group taken with a digital camera and ready at the end of the trip. They will also, for 5 dollars email you a copy. We suggested that they might like to think about making mousemats out of the photos for those of a more technological bent.

We were recommended by the motel to eat at the White Morph restaurant, but on the night we tried it there was a waiting list so we went along the coast to the Green Dolphin. That turned out to be excellent, with the slight exception that the waitress tried to poison Jackie with a sweet containing strawberry despite having being warned that Jackie is allergic to them. Fortunately Jackie realised in time and the incident was laughed off. By coincidence we discovered the next morning that the waitress, Rachael, was the daughter of the couple who ran the motel where we were staying!

Next morning we took a two hour sea fishing trip with Bruce of Dusky Lodge. He took us out to a mark in about 200 ft of water and the three of us, including Sam, a chef from Harrogate who was working his way round the world, started catching fish straight away—sea perch and blue cod. Tackle was a stiff rod with multiplier reel and heavy nylon with a big lead weight and two big hooks on each trace baited with strips of skin and flesh cut from the catch (or in the case of the first few from the previous day's catch). Sadly, after about a half an hour the wind got up and we could not keep the baits on the bottom so we moved inshore and moored to one of Bruce's crayfish pots but even then the wind and tide were so strong that we were dragging the mooring and so caught no more. Bruce was very well equipped with echo sounder, GPS, radio, compass, mobile phone, etc. and the trip was interesting. A highlight of the fishing trip was watching the albatross, black backed and wandering soaring alongside the boat, incredible birds! The fish made an excellent supper back at the motel that night, with a bottle of Kaikoura Chardonnay; the blue cod was marginally tastier than the perch and the boysenberry ice cream to finish with was excellent.

Mike had considered going to swim with the dusky dolphins here but decided that it did not seem such an attractive option as at Akaroa, being on a much larger scale and less personal, as well as being booked up several days ahead; so that idea was shelved.

Friday 17 March, being St Patrick's Day, we felt duty bound to sample the Guinness at the Donegal Inn, about 5 km outside the town. The party had not really started when we arrived at about 6.30 but the music was already deafening and we were cornered by the pub's resident bore so we decided not to stay for the evening.

Kaikoura Museum was interesting and good value for NZ$2 per head. There was a big flood in 1993, the result of heavy rainfall in the hills and interference with the original course of the river. I saw a good book called *Whales and Dolphins of Kaikoura*, by Barbara Todd, but there were none for sale and it is evidently out of print though with the prospect of a reprint shortly. A trip to the Point to try to photograph seals was unsuccessful—there were hardly any about compared with the day before when we had not got the camera with us. Typical!

Friday 19 March saw us heading south from Kaikoura towards Hanmer Springs, a spa and ski resort in the foothills of the Southern Alps. On the way we had to pass Kaikoura airport and Mike could not resist the temptation to have half an hour in a Cessna. The instructor was a young man working up his hours towards an ATPL and he was kind enough to let Mike do all the flying. That put Mike in an unusually good mood, which lasted almost a whole day.

The Hanmer Resort hotel was a bit of a disappointment, but it had been all we could get because there was a big conference on there that weekend. The main drawback was the lack of Sky TV which meant that we could not watch the Super 12 action that night. The hot springs were marvellous and very relaxing and to make up for the lack of Sky we treated ourselves to a slap up dinner at the Old Post Office restaurant, reputed to be the best in town. It was run by a Dutch couple, whose young son was the chef, and lived up to its reputation. One of the best restaurant meals of the whole trip.

Next day, Sunday, we pottered gently down to Christchurch, passing many vintage cars, including proper Bentleys etc. all going north, presumably to or from some rally or other. When we arrived at the motel in Christchurch we discovered that yet again we had got it wrong—no Sky, and the Super 12 and two 5 Nations games on. However one of the Super 12 games, Auckland Blues v Queensland Reds was on Channel 1 but turned out to be a 12 all draw and hardly worth watching.

We liked Christchurch a lot. It is very much a garden city and, like everywhere else we went in New Zealand, uncrowded, relaxed and relaxing, with lots of old world charm. We enjoyed a trip on the City Tram which does a circuit of the sights with a commentary from the driver, very entertaining ('... for the benefit of the Australians amongst you that over there is a car park ...') and good value. Yet more seafood, this time oysters were consumed in the pavement cafés overlooking the river! We also had a very good curry one evening.

The Antarctic Centre, out by the airport, was very well done and absolutely fascinating. We learnt an enormous amount in a short time about a continent that is really not very familiar to us Brits. A must for all visitors.

The Red Bus proved a good way of getting in and out of Christchurch without having to take the car. Every half hour from outside the motel to the Cathedral Square—and no worries about drink/driving.

The next, and last, day we spent the morning at the Royal New Zealand Air Force Museum at Wigram, just outside Christchurch. Wigram no longer has any resident units but is maintained as an operational airfield and there was an exercise involving C-130s etc. going on at the time. The Museum is interesting and well provided with old and bold (look who's talking) and knowledgeable ex-Air Force guides. We asked about Richard Pearse and his reputed first flight before the Wright brothers. There was considerable scepticism about whether he really did achieve it and also about whether the replica of his aircraft on top of the memorial at Waitohi is structurally accurate. Apparently some bits of his original aircraft exist in a museum at Wellington but the opportunity to see those had unfortunately passed.

Near Wigram is another vintage car museum, this one owned by a man and his son who specialise in restorations, and some of the cars are actually for sale, e.g. a restored 1962 Mini Cooper for about £3,000.

Tuesday 23 March. New Zealand Departure Day. Transport arrived on time and Air NZ flight (767-300) left on schedule for the 3 hour leg to Raratonga. One hour on the ground at Raratonga wandering round the very basic terminal on a warm tropical evening listening to Hawaiian entertainers was no pain then another 5 hours on to Honolulu in the same aircraft. 0200 arrival at Honolulu meant that all the airport facilities such as currency exchange were closed and to complete our joy the transport to the hotel was absent. Eventually we shared a taxi with another passenger whose transport from a different company was also not there. After some confusion (there are about 8 different Outrigger hotels in Honolulu) we arrived at ours (Outrigger Reef) at 0400 having had a bellyful of the 'time to spare travel by air' syndrome.

The hotel proved to be excellent, very professionally geared to the needs of holidaymakers, with its own swimming pool and direct access to the beach, although the sea was a bit cool for our by then educated taste. ATI the travel firm refunded our taxi money without question and admitted that they had stopped using the firm that let us down because of their unreliability.

Happy hour (beer $2 a glass) at the poolside bar set us up for a cook-it-yourself supper in one of the several hotel restaurants. Next day we did the obligatory Pearl Harbor tour, including the USS *Arizona* Memorial. Our guide, Brian, proved very knowledgeable and useful in telling us where to sit in the theatre, on the boat and where to go first on the memorial, etc. The memorial is tastefully done and avoids being too morbid, considering that it is built over the sunken battleship which still contains the remains of the 1,100 sailors who died when she went down. The conspiracy theories were explored by Brian, without prejudice, and the occasion gave much food for thought.

That afternoon we wanted to get out of the Waikiki tourist area to see something of the countryside so booked a Rainforest Tour. The guide was a professor who was stuck on transmit and more interested in telling us about introduced species of trees than showing us birds and wildlife. Eventually we did see a few new birds and some mongooses (mongeese?) and to be fair the views over Waikiki were spectacular. Like many places, the Hawaiian islands have suffered from the introduction of non-native species and continue to be threatened by development for tourism etc. Honolulu was well worth visiting, if only as a prime example of fitness for purpose, i.e. tourism.

0300 reveille made for a restrained start to our flight home, especially as once again nothing at the airport was open at that hour. The Air NZ 747-400 left on time for the 5 hour leg to Los Angeles but when we arrived there was an aircraft unserviceable on our gate and the delay of about 45 minutes made the connection pretty tight. However we made it only to find ourselves seated right at the back of the cabin, near the toilets and several small children who spent the night running up and down the aisle. Not the most comfortable of flights, especially since in turbulence the 747 shimmies, which is most pronounced at the back. Still, we made it and Mike's brother David was at Heathrow to greet us back to a grey, cool UK.

And Now!

In retrospect I consider myself lucky that my stroke did not prove fatal as the time I have spent confined to a wheelchair has provided the opportunity to write this memoir which I probably would not have done had I not been disabled.

Looking back as I have I realise how lucky I have been to lead a full and interesting life, blessed with good friends and family who have given me wonderful support, particularly over the last three difficult years.

We continue to live in Wylye and are able to go out in our wheelchair-accessible Renault Kangoo which is called Pat as it is bright red and looks like a post office van, although no black and white cat!

It was with great pleasure that we were able to welcome about 60 family and friends to celebrate our Golden Wedding Anniversary in May last year and so life goes on.

List of Planes Flown

[figures in square brackets are after the loss of right eye]. A total of 42 different fixed wing planes and 7 helicopters. 3,316 hours total, [1,209] after the loss of my eye. Hours rounded up to the nearest hour.

Andover C1 and Andover CC2
[161 hours]
Powered by two Rolls Royce Dart turbo prop engines, the Andover was being bought by the RAF in two military versions based on the Hawker Siddeley 748. The CC2 which arrived at Boscombe first was destined for use as transport for VIPs and the Queens Flight. The C1 was adapted for rear loading of freight and had a kneeling undercarriage to enable height adjustment of the rear loading ramp. They were both similar to fly but the C1 used an interesting short landing technique consisting of pulling reverse prop pitch in the flare to minimise the landing run.

Argosy
29 hours and [255 hours]
Built by Whitworth Gloster Aviation and with four Rolls Royce Dart 101 engines the Argosy was a large transport aircraft which was used for freight, passengers and parachutists, also parachute supply drops.

A pleasant and easy aircraft to fly the Dart turboprop engines had a useful water/methanol injection system to boost maximum power for short periods. Many of my hours on the Argosy were in one fitted out by Smiths for auto-landing trials.

Auster 9 No. 672
5 hours
Built by Taylorcraft and powered by a de Havilland Gipsy Major engine.

One day I found myself scheduled to fly a photo trial in the Auster AOP 9 fitted with a photopod under the wing. The pod was adjustable for angle so that the photos could be taken vertically or obliquely. The angle of the oblique was sighted through a chinagraphed marking on the Perspex side window. Until I flew the Auster I thought that adverse aileron yaw only existed in ETPS text books but I then found it existed in a big way in reality, perhaps because the aircraft had been fitted with extra-large ailerons to increase the rate of roll. It was left to me to decide what should be photographed for the trial and the idea struck me to photograph some of the local hostelries and I then went around the establishments with the photos and traded them for a pint of beer or three!

Beagle Basset
[19 hours]
The RAF version of the Beagle B206 was bought as a light communications aircraft with the concept of flying V-bomber crews around the UK. A low wing, twin-engine monoplane with retractable undercarriage, the B206 already had a civil clearance so the Boscombe Down trials were simplified. It turned out to have the odd problem such as the propeller tips hitting the ground whilst taxiing. The Basset was a pleasant little aeroplane and after its CA release went into squadron service at RAF Northolt. Later on a Basset was converted to have a variable stability system installed which was used as part of the ETPS fleet until it left the service in late 2014

Belfast
[1 hour 40 minutes]
Built by Short Brothers and Harland in Belfast and delivered in 1966 to the RAF it was the first military transport with a fully automatic landing system.

Blackburn Beverley
41 hours and [62 hours]
Manufactured by the Blackburn and General Aircraft Company and powered by four Bristol Centaurus 273 engines the Beverley was at the time the largest aircraft in service with the RAF.

The Beverley was a pleasant aircraft to fly with harmonious controls; however it had a thirst for engine oil and sometimes had to be topped up in flight. It also had a reverse pitch propeller and when taxiing back in reverse you had to remember not to brake hard or it would sit down on its tail!

Bristol Freighter
30 minutes
Built by the Bristol Aircraft Company and powered by two Bristol Hercules 734 engines.

E Squadron at Boscombe Down had a Bristol Freighter used for carrying freight and as a 'type Hog' I took the opportunity to get checked out in it. It must have been unexceptional as I have no particular memories of it.

Bulldog
[63 hours]
The Bulldog was bought by the RAF as a replacement for the long serving Chipmunk. It was designed and initially built by the ill-fated Beagle Aircraft Company, later versions were built by Scottish Aviation. The type was first delivered to RAF Little Rissington in 1973 and early versions were not capable of performing the full range of Aerobatics, but later versions were fully aerobatic.

I first flew the Bulldog at Little Rissington during a self-imposed spell of refresher flying before taking over as station commander in late 1973. It was a pleasant and forgiving little aircraft but of limited performance, its big advantage over the Chipmunk was cabin heating which did away with the need for bunny suits. The tricycle undercarriage was seen by some QFIs as a retrograde step.

Canberra B2
26 hours and [2½ hours]
The English Electric Canberra was powered by two Rolls Royce Avon engines and was a light bomber with a crew of three.

I was involved in the 'snatch' trials at Boscombe Down carried out with a converted Interdictor Canberra. The trial consisted of picking up a target hanging by a rope looped between two poles with hook fixed below the rear fuselage of the Canberra. This meant flying at a height of 10 feet above the ground with undercarriage up and when the target was caught climbing steeply on full power and a little flap selected. This worked successfully in getting the target airborne without it dragging along the ground.

Chipmunk
36 hours and [367 hours]
Built by the de Havilland Aircraft Company and powered by a Gipsy Major 8 engine.

A two-seater trainer which was the mainstay of basic flying training and the university air squadrons for many years. The Chipmunk was somewhat underpowered and could not maintain height in Aerobatics. Another problem was that it had no cockpit heating and so we were all issued with woolly 'bunny suits' these were very bulky and we all looked like Michelin men trying to burst out of our flying suits.

Comet
[8½ hours]
I did two trips in the second pilot seat of the Boscombe Down Comet and found it easy to fly despite a complicated hydraulic system.

Devon
55 hours and [8 hours]
Built by de Havilland and powered by two Gipsy Queen Engines.

The Devon was an RAF version of the civil Dove aircraft and was used as a transport and communications base. During testing at Boscombe Down it was concluded that the single engine performance might be marginal especially bearing in mind that it was frequently used as VIP transport. The Devon could not maintain a height over 1 500 ft in hot weather trials and in the event it was re-engined.

Dominie
12 hours
Built by Hawker Siddeley and bought by the RAF as a navigation trainer it was a military version of the Hawker Siddeley 125 carrying a crew of two plus two pupils. Because it already had a civil clearance the acceptance trials at Boscombe Down were almost a formality. It was an easy and pleasant plane to fly with no asymmetric problems because of the placement of the engines close to the centre line.

Gnat T1
[28 hours]
Originally designed and built by Folland Aviation who were taken over by Hawker Siddeley in the big revision of industry structure, the Gnat was a pleasant little two-seat, dual control high performance fighter type aircraft. It was a successor to the Folland Midge light fighter and was used as a jet trainer and from 1965 to 1979 was for a time the aircraft of the Red Arrows.

Harvard
45 minutes and [3 hours]
The RAF standard advanced trainer for many years and was the last propeller driven advanced trainer until replaced by the Vampire T11. The Harvard remained in service for many years with the university air squadrons and A&AEE in a photo chase role. It produced a characteristic rasping noise, caused; it is said, by the propeller being

directly driven by the engine resulting in high propeller tip speeds. A
pleasing aircraft to fly and good at the photo chase job because as the
seats were in tandem the photographer in the rear seat could operate
on both side of the aircraft. As a tail-wheel aircraft it needed careful
handling and many were the ground loops performed by Jet Jocks
unfamiliar with tail wheelers.

Hastings
55 hours and [52 hours]
A large and heavy tail-wheel aircraft which between them did nothing
to recommend it to me! My worst fears were eventually realised at
Lajes Airfield in the Azores where we left the runway in a strong cross
wind and damaged the underside of the tail plane which delayed us
for some days whilst a repair party flew out from Boscombe. The only
saving grace was that, as co-pilot, I was not flying the aircraft at the
time. I never checked out in the Hastings, nor did I want to!

Hawk
[1 hour]
When the Red Arrows took delivery of the Hawk in 1980 they came
out to Cyprus for their pre-season training and I took the opportunity
to take a trip with their Wing Commander Black. The Hawk was an
easy and slippery little plane to fly and very well suited to its training
and aerobatic role.

Hercules
[4½ hours]
2 hours 50 minutes of this was on a visit to the US Air Force Edwards
Base in 1965 I was offered a ride down to Travis and back and jumped
at the opportunity. The two pilots flying the plane took pity on me
as I sat in the cockpit looking forlorn and allowed me to have a fly.
On returning to UK I wrote, from memory the report at Appendix
D and handed it in to Boscombe Down saying very clearly that this
is the plane we should buy rather than the Belfast which was under
consideration at the time.

Hunter F1
25 hours
Single-seater short range interceptor fighter manufactured by the Hawker Aircraft Company with a Rolls Royce Avon 104 or 107 engine.

Hunter F4
38 hours
Single-seater similar to the F1 but powered by the Avon 113 or 114 engine and with a larger fuel capacity.

Hunter F6
204 hours
A similar single-seat interceptor day fighter but with the more powerful Rolls Royce Avon 203 engine giving 10,000 lb of thrust.

Hunter T7
23 hours [18 hours]
A two-seater advanced trainer built by Hawker Aircraft Company and powered by the Rolls Royce Avon 122 engine giving 8,000 lb thrust.

The Hunter was my favourite aircraft of all, although the F1 particularly, suffered from a shortage of fuel load which limited its operational capability to around 30 minutes. The later F4, and F6 had an increased fuel capacity and a larger engine, which while it increased the operational envelope, gave slightly reduced performance. The Hunter was capable of going supersonic in a dive. The Hunter 6 is perhaps best known as the aeroplane of No. 111 Squadron, Black Arrows aerobatic team.

Javelin 5
2 hours
Built by the Gloster Aircraft Company and powered by two Bristol Siddeley Sapphire engines the Javelin was a two-seat all weather fighter.

I scrounged a trip in the Javelin because it was a type I had not flown before. It handled like an overgrown Meteor, not outstanding in any way although very gentlemanly.

Jaguar

[45minutes]

The Anglo-French Jaguar powered by two Rolls Royce turbofan engines was originally envisaged as an advanced trainer. In the event it was introduced to service as a low level bomber optimised for low level cruise. I found it rather sluggish and seemingly underpowered. Its place as an advanced trainer was eventually filled by the Hawk, a more sensible single engine design.

Jet Provost

[3 hours]

The Jet Provost replaced the Piston Provost as the RAF's basic trainer in 1957. A two-seat plane with a tricycle undercarriage and Armstrong Siddeley Viper engine, the JP was an unremarkable basic trainer which saw many years of service with flying training schools and the final version the T5 went to Central Flying School in 1969.

Lightning

25 minutes and [30 minutes]

Built by English Electric the Lightning was the last in a line of British interceptor fighters. Early versions suffered from the traditional British malady of lack of fuel, in later F6 version this was remedied by the installation of two over-wing fuel tanks. The Lightning was the first British fighter to be supersonic in level flight. An interesting aircraft to fly whose turning performance relied more on engine thrust than aerodynamics.

Meteor T7

12 hours

Built by the Gloster Aircraft Company and powered by two Rolls Royce Derwent engines. The first dual-control jet trainer to go into service with the RAF.

Meteor F8

102 hours

Similar to the T7, but a single-seater day fighter.

Meteor NF14
10 hours [112 hours]
Similar to previous versions of the Meteor, a two-seat night fighter. The Meteor 14 had power assisted controls and although it was heavier and less responsive than the 7 or 8. All the Meteors were very gentlemanly aircraft.

Pembroke
17 hours and [2 hours]
The Hunting Percival Pembroke was powered by two Avon Leonides 127 engines.

The Pembroke was in many ways similar to the Devon although with more powerful engines. It was used mainly for photo reconnaissance and the Boscombe Down plane had a 'Sky shouter' loudspeaker fitted with which crowds on the ground could be addressed. I always wanted to fly over Stonehenge on a solstice night and shout at the Druids, sadly never got to do it.

Phantom
[2½ hours]
An hour of which was a familiarisation flight with Squadron Leader Steve Nichols who had been one of my students at Oxford University Air Squadron when he came on detachment to Cyprus with his squadron. The Phantom struck me most forcefully at wall to wall buffet!

Pioneer
20 minutes
Built by Scottish Aviation Ltd as a five-seat casualty and communication aircraft powered by an Alvis Leonides 520 hp engine.

In November 1963 I did a familiarisation flight with Master Engineer Thomas as co-pilot. I can't remember why E Squadron had a Pioneer but it may well have been that some radio trials were needed and no other squadron wanted to do. I was told that the recommended soft landing threshold speed was 28 knots. I decided to try a soft landing but did not succeed in getting the speed below 30 knots which seemed to me to be a stalling speed accustomed as I was to jet fighters

Provost T1
217 hours, 136 hours solo mainly in basic training but also at ETPS
Two-seat basic trainer manufactured by Hunting Percival and powered
by a 550 hp Avon Leonides engine.

A pleasant, easy to fly basic trainer with a decently powerful engine
unlike its contemporary the Chipmunk which was underpowered.

Valetta
17 hours and [11 hours]
A tailwheel predecessor of the Varsity used at Boscombe Down for
freight carriage and parachute drops; an unremarkable aircraft to fly
but because of the tailwheel configuration it required care on landing.

Vampire FB5
55 hours
Originally a single-seater fighter aircraft but later the advanced jet
trainer, manufactured by de Havilland Aircraft Co. Ltd and powered
by a de Havilland Goblin 1 turbo jet engine.

Vampire FB9
Similar to the FB5
42 hours

Vampire T11
*1,069 hours, 106 dual during jet training. Total 1070 hours plus [30
minutes] at CFS*
Similar to the previous Vampires, based on the night fighter version,
but with a widened cock pit to seat two side by side with dual controls;
powered by a de Havilland Goblin 35.

The T11 was heavier than the single-seaters before it and did not
have as good a performance, although the more powerful engine
helped. It was fitted with ejection seats and as all the Vampires there
was a considerable amount of wood in the construction, hence the
jokes about woodworm rather than metal fatigue!

Varsity
8 hours dual
Built by Vickers Armstrong and powered by two Bristol Hercules engines with a tricycle undercarriage. The Varsity was a version of the Valletta used mainly for navigation training and was somewhat pedestrian to fly after the fighters I was used to.

Viscount
4 hours
Built by Vickers Armstrong with four Rolls Royce Dart turbo prop engines, the plane was used to ferry the ETPS course around.

These Aircraft also figure in my log book on a 'one off' basis often thanks to the kindness of fellow pilots when I visited foreign Air Forces: Nimrod *5 hours*; Shackleton *2 hours*; OV10 Bronco; T2A Buckeye; A3B Sky warrior; Macchi MB326; CA25 Winjeel; CT4 Airtrainer, and the Motor Faulke powered glider.

Helicopters Flown

Whirlwind

[57 hours]

When I discovered that the only resident aircraft I would have as AOC Cyprus were Whirlwind Helicopters I arranged for a short familiarisation course at RAF Ternhill. The course was useful but was not designed to send one solo, I eventually achieved my first solo flight at Akrotiri Cyprus courtesy of 84 Squadron.

We had a very convenient Helipad at the bottom of the garden at Flagstaff House and I continued to fly the Whirlwind while in Cyprus including trips up country and flights with visiting VIPs including the chief of the air staff,

I also flew several other helicopters including the Dragonfly, Sea King, Alouette, Iroquos, AH15 Cobra, Gazelle, but did not check out on them

Appendices

Appendix A

Dick Turpin is probably the most legendary highwayman of all time, and his rapid flight from London to York is the most famous part of this legend. Mention the name of Turpin to most people, and they will tell you he was a daring and dashing rogue who famously rode this trip of two hundred miles on his faithful mare, Black Bess, in less than fifteen hours. In so doing, Turpin actually got to York before news of his misdemeanours in London. Tests on horses that specialise in endurance events have shown that this would not have been possible.

Various inns that still stand along the original route of the A1 (at the time called the Great North Road, the main road connecting the north of England to the south), such as the Roebuck Inn, Stevenage, claim that Turpin ate there that night, or stopped off there for a brief respite for his horse. If he had really stopped at every inn that makes such claims then he would not have had time to ride anywhere. Yet the legend persists.

Appendix B

F/L Williams

From:- Group Captain A.W. Heward, O.B.E.,D.F.C.,A.F.C.,R.A.F.

FIN/2214/4/Org

Royal Air Force,
Finningley,
Doncaster,
Yorkshire.

20th September, 1961

I must write and congratulate you on the excellent formation aerobatics by your three Vampires on Saturday. It was one of the highlights of our display, the finale being most impressive.

2. Thank you also for the Varsity which we had in the Static Aircraft display.

3. It was most disappointing that the winds were too strong to permit the performance by Flight Lieutenant Bridson. We had given this item a lot of local publicity and the crowd were quite disappointed. However, I hope that he can come next year.

4. I should be grateful if you will convey my sincere thanks and congratulations to the pilots of your acrobatic team on a very spirited and polished performance.

Yours sincerely,
Signed: A.W. Heward

Group Captain G.F. Reid, D.F.C.,R.A.F.
Royal Air Force,
Cranwell,
Lincolnshire

Appendix C

From: Group Captain A.D. Mitchell, C.V.O., D.F.C., A.F.C., A.D.C.

Telephone No. :—
COTTESMORE 241.
Extn. _____290_____

Correspondence on the subject of this letter should be addressed to the COMMANDING OFFICER and should quote the reference :—

_____COT/C.140/11/Air_____

Your ref. _____

ROYAL AIR FORCE,
COTTESMORE,
OAKHAM,
RUTLAND.

22 September, 1961

Dear Williams,

Many thanks for your help last week-end in our "Open Day" programme.

Despite the high wind 34,000 people attended. I have received a large number of letters saying how much they enjoyed the show which has also been praised by the press.

Please accept my sincere thanks for your participation.

Yours sincerely,

A.D. Mitchell

Flight Lieutenant Williams,
    Officers' Mess,
        Royal Air Force,
            Cranwell,
                Sleaford,
                    Lincolnshire

Appendix D

This is the report that I handed in to Boscombe Down on my return from our trip to America and I hope that it had some part in the RAF eventually purchasing the H130.

PILOT'S REPORT ON FLIGHT IN H.C.130H

1. Introduction

   Sqn Ldr M. R. Williams was allowed to fly an H.C.130H for one sortie while at Edwards AFB California. The following report was written from memory as, because the flying was on an 'unofficial' basis, no notes could be taken in the air and the writer was asked not to report officially upon the aircraft.

2. Conditions relevant to the tests

   2.1 Aerodynamic Condition

   The aircraft was a standard production model H.C.130H which was in the Rescue version of the C.130H. It carried no payload but had an empty 11,000 lb. over load fuel tank fitted in the fuselage, and provision for a further 11,000 lb. tank to be fitted. With both these tanks full it was capable of an endurance approaching 24 hours. It was designed to be cruised on 2 engines in the search configuration. The aircraft seemed fairly new.

   2.2 Weight and centre of Gravity

   Take-off weight was 110,000 lbs. max. Normal AUW was 145,000 lbs. and max. overload AVW was 175,000 lbs. C of G was not ascertained.

2.3 Weather Time and Place

One flight of 2 hours 50 minutes duration was made from Edwards AFB to Travis AFB and return on 22nd September 1965. Passengers were being carried which severely limited the amount of test flying which could be attempted. Weather was fine with a surface OAT of +30° C. Winds were light and there was no cloud.

3. Tests Made

3.1 Cockpit Assessment
3.2 Start Up
3.3 Taxying
3.4 Take-off and Climb
3.5 General Flying
3.6 Low Flying
3.7 Stalling
3.8 Asymmetric
3.9 Descent
3.10 Circuit and Landing

4 Results of Tests
4.1 Cockpit Assessment
The cockpit layout was generally good and it seemed that all the instruments etc. needed by the two pilots were fairly accessible. A lot of the roof panel was not accessible to the two pilots but the flight engineer looked after this. The flying controls were well placed and it was comfortable to fly the aircraft with one hand on the control column and the other on the throttles. The flight deck was reasonably roomy and the seats were comfortable being adjustable for height value and fore–aft position. The flight instruments although of American pattern, were straight forward and easily read but on the centre panel there were a lot of similar sized engine instruments which,

as well as essential things like T.I.T and R.P.M., included oil contents gauges for each of the engines. View from the cockpit was excellent and downward vision was available almost to the vertical. There was also a window in the roof over each pilot's head. R/T reception on UHF was clear and American UHF R/T seemed clearer than does British.

4.2 Start Up

Engine Start-up, which was carried out by the captain, appeared simple by an automatic cycle but for some reason No. 3 engine faded out a few seconds after starting normally, and had to be restarted. Checks did not appear too lengthy but may have been shortened by the very experienced captain.

4.3 Taxying

Not much power was required to start moving, the aircraft being fairly light. The toe-brakes were a little 'sharp' in action. A Harvard-type parking brake was fitted which did not engage until the toe brakes were fully depressed to the stops. The nose-wheel steering, by a hand wheel was good though so low geared by British standards that a knob was fitted on the rim of the hand-wheel to facilitate 'twirling'. A lateral rocking of the aircraft was felt while cornering, presumably a feature of a narrow-track undercarriage and this rocking was also noticed on the landing run. Reverse pitch could be used at will for speed control and the normal method was to use only two throttles for taxying.

4.4 Take off and Climb

The pre-take off checks were straight forward and a rolling start was made. The 1st pilot's left hand was on the nose-wheel steering and his right hand on the throttles up to 90 knots when the left hand was transferred to the stick. At a weight of 110,000 we rotated at 110 knots with a fairly large backward movement of the stick but with a light one-handed pull force. In fact the aircraft did not need more than one hand on the stick at any time during the sortie. Acceleration was rapid and little runway was used though the OAT was +30° C. The USAF does not appear to use a safety speed or to use the terms V_1 or V_2 but had a speed called Minimum Control speed, which is defined as 'the minimum speed at which limited control of the airplane in flight can be maintained by the pilot if an outboard engine abruptly fails.......'. Graphs available for the C.130.A show this speed at +30° C, Sea Level, and 110,000 lbs to be 10 knots below VR. The undercarriage was retracted without noticeable change of trim and flap was brought up from 50°, again without noticeable change of trim. Climbing speed for the weight was 180 knots, which gave an initial rate of climb of over 2,000 ft/min. Speed stability in the climb was good and over 1,000 ft/min. rate of climb was still showing when the aircraft levelled out at 10,500 ft. Power was then reduced to give a cruise speed of about 240 knots.

4.5   General Flying

Control harmony was good and forces generally light though a considerable change of longitudinal trim with power was evident, also for some reason which was not apparent there was a change of rudder trim with power. The electrical elevator trimmer on the stick was powerful and needed care in use. Aileron and rudder trims on the central console were also electrically operated and effective though not so powerful as the elevator trimmer. Stability appeared good, a selected speed being easily held and trim changes with speed were in the normal sense. The only two criticisms of the controls were (i) that aileron response at low speeds was rather sluggish though the ailerons remained effective, and (ii) that it was a little difficulty to maintain correct directional trim due to the high rudder power in cruising flight. The controls were all hydraulically boosted with a standby hydraulic system. It was claimed that the C.130.A could be controlled in manual by the combined efforts of the trimmers and both pilots but manual was regarded as an emergency condition and was not practised.

4.6   Low Flying

Some low flying was carried out in the Sierra Nevada Mountains up to 14,500 ft. ASL and the aircraft was found to be very pleasant in this role. The visibility from the cockpit was excellent, the manoeuvrability good, and an ample reserve of power was available to climb if necessary to avoid rising ground.

4.7   Stalling

Two stalls were tried one clean and one with full flap.

4.7.1 Stall Clean

Power was reduced to idling at 17,000 feet and a mild airframe buffet started 15 knots above the stall. The buffet did not get very pronounced and the stall itself was mild with a clean nose drop from a nose high position. Stalling speed was about 110 knots, there was no wing drop and recovery was normal.

4.7.2 Stall with full flap

At 17,000 ft there was a restriction on undercarriage lowering so approach power and full flap were used to simulate a stall in the landing configuration. There was less preliminary buffet and the stalling speed was 90 knots. At the stall itself the buffet became more marked and the starboard wing dropped but was held with aileron. Recovery was normal. No artificial stall waring system was fitted.

4.8   Asymmetric

No. 4 engine was feathered in cruising flight at 13,000 ft. and 250 knots. Speed fell by about 30 knots. After feathering it was some time before the engine could be unfeathered because the T.I.T had to be allowed to fall to 100° C. No further asymmetric flight was made, due to passengers on board. The lateral rocking on the runway mentioned in 4.3. might well have been accentuated with asymmetric power. It is of interest to note that in the Flight Manual for the C.130. A there was a warning that the aircraft became directionally unstable in the power approach and climb configurations, above 200° of sideslip. 'The instability occurs when approximately 80% of full rudder pedal travel is applied with the airplane yawed and banked to maintain a constant heading. The airplane will float to a 40° or more sideslip angle with no change in rudder position and a decrease in rudder pedal force'. Investigation of this phenomenon in the H.C.130H was not attempted!

4.9   Descent

A speed of 250 knots with throttle well back gave a rate of descent of about 2,000 ft/min., with stable speed holding.

4.10 Circuit and Landing

The circuit was joined at 1,000 ft., below 180 knots which was the limiting speed for 50° flap and undercarriage lowering. 5oo flap was selected giving a transient nose up trim change. Undercarriage lowering produced no appreciable trim change. The turn off the downwind leg was made at 145 knots and at the 90° position full flap was selected with speed 135 knots. This produced a nose-down trim change and a 'ballooning' of the aircraft. The target threshold speed was 115 and at this speed there was ample margin above the stall. The captain advised the use of a trickle of power until touchdown and this was used but in the light wind conditions it was not felt to be essential. The aircraft was exceptionally easy to land, being stable in the approach configuration and having good thrust response. The fact that only one hand was needed on the stick left the other free to operate the throttles which made for finer speed control than can be achieved in some British aircraft which need two hands on the stick in the last stages of the approach. Full flap did not give all that much extra drag and it was felt that it would be fairly easy to arrive at the threshold too fast. After touchdown the left hand was transferred to the nose wheel steering and a simple up-and-back movement of the throttles gave ground idle, further backward movement past a detent giving reverse pitch. About 60° engine power was available in reverse which did not seem to give a lot of deceleration though no doubt the addition of full braking would give acceptable stopping distances.

5. Conclusions

    The H.C.130H proved to be a very easy and pleasant aeroplane to fly and at the weight as flown (35,000 lbs below max. AUW), possessed an exceptionally good performance.

(M. R. Williams)
Squadron Leader.

Boscombe Down.
25th October 1965

Appendix E

High Flight
John Gillespie Magee, Jr

Oh! I have slipped the surly bonds of earth,
And danced the skies on laughter-silvered wings;
Sunward I've climbed, and joined the tumbling mirth
Of sun-split clouds,—and done a hundred things
You have not dreamed of—Wheeled and soared and swung
High in the sunlit silence. Hov'ring there
I've chased the shouting wind along, and flung
My eager craft through footless halls of air...
Up, up the long, delirious, burning blue
I've topped the wind-swept heights with easy grace
Where never lark or even eagle flew—
And, while with silent lifting mind I've trod
The high untrespassed sanctity of space,
Put out my hand, and touched the face of God.